Do W

Economic inequality?

The Future of Capitalism series

Danny Dorling, *Do We Need Economic Inequality?*
Steve Keen, *Can We Avoid Another Financial Crisis?*
Malcolm Sawyer, *Can the Euro be Saved?*

Danny Dorling

———————

Do We Need
Economic Inequality?

polity

First published in 2018 by Polity Press
Reprinted 2017, 2018

Polity Press
65 Bridge Street
Cambridge CB2 1UR, UK

Polity Press
101 Station Landing, Suite 300
Medford, MA 02155, USA

ISBN-13: 978-1-5095-1654-4
ISBN-13: 978-1-5095-1655-1(pb)

A catalogue record for this book is available from the British Library.

Typeset in 11/15 Sabon by Servis Filmsetting Limited, Stockport, Cheshire
Printed and bound in the UK by CPI Group (UK) Ltd, Croydon

The publisher has used its best endeavours to ensure that the URLs for external websites referred to in this book are correct and active at the time of going to press. However, the publisher has no responsibility for the websites and can make no guarantee that a site will remain live or that the content is or will remain appropriate.

Every effort has been made to trace all copyright holders, but if any have been inadvertently overlooked the publisher will be pleased to include any necessary credits in any subsequent reprint or edition.

For further information on Polity, visit our website: politybooks.com

To Alison Dorling

Contents

Acknowledgements

Thanks are due to three anonymous referees, and Will Davies, David Dorling, Aniko Horvath and Terry Wrigley for comments on various drafts of this book. George Owers at Polity commissioned the book and also commented extensively and very positively on both earlier and later drafts. Rachel Moore very competently saw it through production, correcting many errors, and Caroline Burkitt proofread all the text. Miles Corak of the University of Ottawa, Andy Hood of the Institute for Fiscal Studies, Michael Clemence and Gideon Skinner of Ipsos Mori, and Peter Lindert of the University of California kindly gave permission for their figures to be redrawn for use in this book; and Adam Keefe drew up the first draft of figure 5.2. Ailsa Allan kindly drew up the final versions of Figures 5.1, 5.2, 5.3, 6.2, 6.3 and 8.1. Many others have pointed me

Acknowledgements

towards much of the new material shown in these pages in various correspondences over recent years. I am grateful for a large number of emails and suggestions and apologize for not dutifully recording all this correspondence – often from people I had never before met. If you recognize a reference to a piece of pertinent information you have sent to me – thank you ever so much! As always, all help is gratefully received but all errors are my responsibility.

1

Bell Curves

The person who's poor and contented is rich enough.
But infinite riches are nothing to someone who's
always afraid he'll be poor. God, help us not be
jealous.

Iago, Othello, Act 3 Scene 3[1]

Shakespeare's England was not a rich country. By the
year 1600 the average income in England would buy
you the equivalent of $1,000 (£800) a year today,
not much more than $2.50 a day (£2).[2] Worldwide
over 3 billion people still survive on around $2.50 a
day. We are still living in Shakespearean times.

Four hundred years ago Gross Domestic Product
(GDP) per capita in Holland was 2.5 times greater
than in England. The Dutch were the first people
in the modern era to begin to grow rich on trade.
The British were the second, but in both cases these
riches were amassed by just a few.

By 1800, when adjusted for inflation, the UK's GDP per head had doubled to $2,000 (£1,600) a year per person and inequalities rose to the highest they had ever been.[3] GDP more than doubled in the next century to reach $4,500 by 1900. It then rose abruptly to reach $8,000 by 1957, $16,000 by 1990; then slowing to peak at $25,000 (£20,000) in 2007, after which it fell, only recovering to its 2007 level by 2017.

The capitalist transformation created a wider *spread* of incomes and a greater *concentration* of wealth than ever seen before. Across Europe the wealth share of the poorest 90% of people halved between 1600 and 1800 and then halved again by 1900.[4] Today only a very small minority of households in the UK receive an income above the average GDP per person, or have above-mean-average wealth. The bottom fifth of households currently receive, on average, about the equivalent income of the average British person a century ago.[5] We tend to overestimate both progress and stability.

There is nothing stable about a distribution of income inequality that fluctuates as wildly as that shown in figure 1.1. Between 1984 and 1990 the ratio of the top to bottom UK income quintiles rose from 4.0 to 6.4. This happened for political reasons: 1984 was the year in which the last great

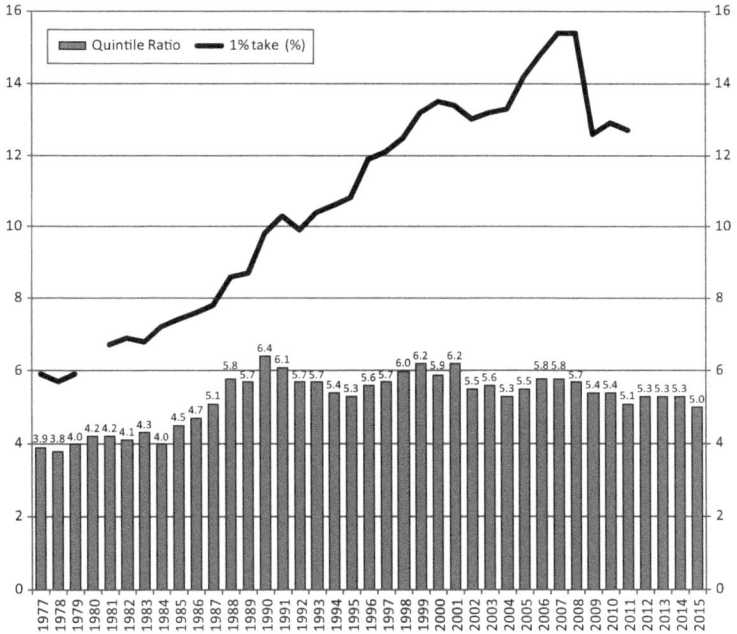

Figure 1.1 Household income inequality, quintile ratio 1977–2015, and 1% take 1977–2012, UK

Source: ONS (2017) *Household Disposable Income and Inequality in the UK: top fifth/bottom fifth excluding the incomes of the best-off 1% of households, which rose during this period.* The take of the 1% is shown as a separate line, derived from the World Wealth and Income Database, http://wid.world/.

Note: Quintile ratio is the ratio of the average income of the best-off fifth of households to the average income of the worse-off fifth of households.

3

miners' strike occurred, they lost; 1990 was the year when Mrs Thatcher finally resigned, when she lost.

Mrs Thatcher was an advocate of inequality. She believed ability was distributed along a bell curve in which a few people were very unable, most were ordinary, and just a few were super-able. She talked of the super-able, of encouraging some of our children to grow taller than others, like 'tall poppies' and of how no one admired a man who travelled by public transport. It was during her pre-miership that the top 1% began to take more and more, as she thought they should, and as figure 1.1 illustrates. As yet we don't know if their take only temporarily fell after 2010.

One problem with discussing inequality is that people cannot easily comprehend the entirety of what is being talked about. Consider the current global distribution of income inequality and con-sider all the people on earth today. A graph that did justice to the actual numbers of people and the degree of income disparity seen worldwide would have to be too huge to draw in this book.

Worldwide, the top 1% receives so much that they make the average earnings of the remaining 99% appear insignificant. The top 0.1% takes so much as to make the earnings of the otherwise best-off 9.9% look insignificant. Figure 1.2 uses a

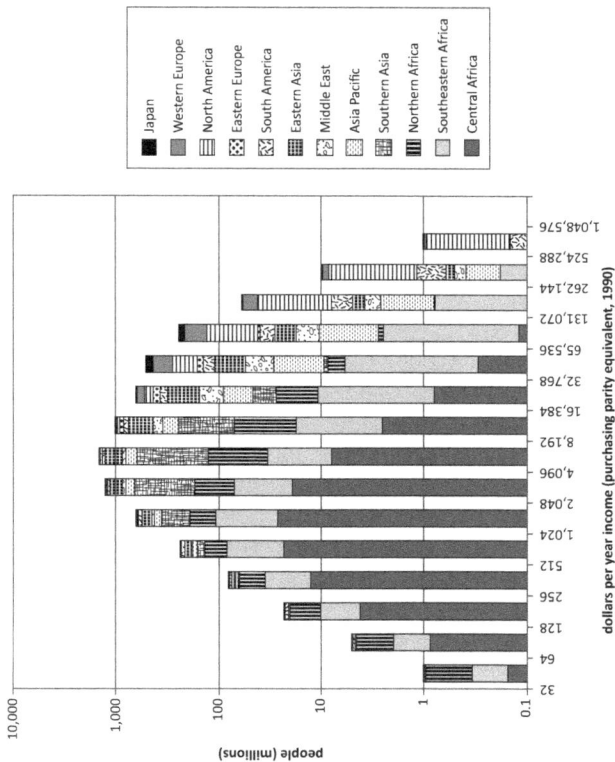

Figure 1.2 Worldwide distribution of income per person by region, year 2000

Source: Dorling, D. and Pritchard, J. (2010) The geography of poverty, inequality and wealth in the UK and abroad: because enough is never enough, *Applied Spatial Analysis and Policy*, 3, 2–3, pp. 81–106, table 1, p. 102.

5

mathematical trick, a log-log scale, to show global income inequality, appearing as if we were all part of a normal curve. This is the key graph of global economic inequality and it is highly misleading.

Currently the world is simultaneously becoming both more equal and more unequal. It is becoming more equal because inequalities between countries fell recently. However, the world is also becoming more unequal when the desperate lives of those who are poorest of all are considered. Far fewer can now rely on self-sufficiency from farming. Housing has become a commodity rather than a right or inheritance in so much more of the world. And a tiny number of extremely rich people have also recently become much richer.

We now know that most of the infamous sixty to eighty people who have as much wealth as the poorest half of humanity are still becoming richer. So much so that by updating their methodology in 2017 Oxfam could claim that just eight billionaires now owned that much.[6] For all practical purposes those eight individuals might as well have infinite riches. They can buy almost anything they desire, but still all of them fear giving too much away. Any who *did* give more away would cease to be in the group. No one individual is *forced* to be in it.

Many philanthropists give with one hand while legitimizing the exploitation that made them rich with their other hand. They argue that their giving is necessary because governments do not spend correctly, as if only they have the super-human powers to see where money is best directed. Governments have less to spend when the richest are effectively taxed so little and grow so very wealthy.

Bell curves, such as that shown in figure 1.2, have been used to depict income inequality because they give the misleading impression that income is distributed on the basis of a 'natural', random variation, which serves the interests of those who want to justify inequality. However, humans have no evolutionary mechanism whereby they produce just a few super-valuable individuals with the rest being people of relatively little or minimal value.

Bell curves describe the distribution of random error very well, or variation around an average height or weight, which is why they are so popular in the physical sciences. But they are not a good description of the natural social relationships between human beings, of our ability and worth. And we are not rewarded as if our worth were distributed along a bell curve. Instead, at times of greatest exploitation the distribution of income becomes extremely uneven, so extreme that it is only by taking the logarithm of both the population and income that the curve shown in the figure will appear remotely bell shaped.

The income distribution of the world shown in figure 1.2 is a completely false bell curve. A curve that is made to look bell shaped through the use of two log scales. Each bar in the graph represents people who receive in real terms twice as much money per year as the group to the left of them. Try to imagine having to live on a quarter of your current income, two bars to the left, or having four times your current income, two bars to the right. It is unthinkable. The six bars that vary between $1,000 and $33,000 a year represent nearly 80% of people in the world. The five left-most bars represent people in extreme poverty.

Bell curves came to be associated with the study of inequality just over 120 years ago when the British Empire was at its peak.[7] In 'leading nations' notions of inevitable inequalities in ability were useful myths for justifying great inequalities, both within Britain and for justifying the subjugations of others living in its colonies, areas that are today most prominent to the left in the graph in figure 1.2. Inequality is determined by factors of power and politics that aren't random, but can be multiplicative when not controlled – those who have most get more and more, until the expropriating trend changes – and it always, eventually, has to change and does always eventually change.

In July 2016 UK Members of Parliament were issued with a report on inequality that concluded with an earlier version of the graph shown in figure 1.3.[8] The text above the graph said that the UK had a higher level of income inequality than *most* other European countries, but lower than the United States. That was presumably meant to suggest that levels of inequality in the UK were somehow OK. But the UK actually reported higher inequality than *any other* European country at that time! Since then inequality in Estonia has risen slightly above that in the UK, as shown in the figure reproduced here using the latest data. Figure 1.3 also shows levels of inequality to be below their most recent peak in two thirds of OECD countries.

There are many ways of measuring inequality. We know that the confusing Gini measure, the one used in figure 1.3, can theoretically produce identical results from very different patterns of income distribution.[9] However, all the commonly used measures of inequality usually end up ranking countries in roughly the same order.

Countries where the 1% takes the most, such as the USA and UK, where they took 17% and 15%

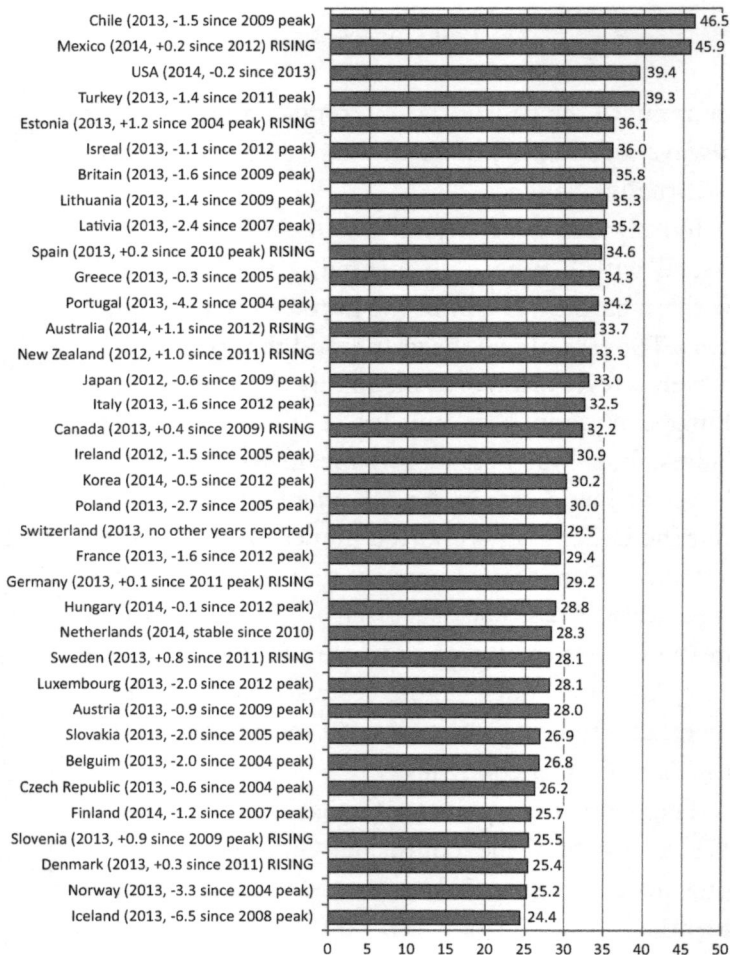

Figure 1.3 Income inequality in OECD countries, 2012–2014, Gini coefficient

Source: McGuinness, F. (2016) *Income Inequality in the UK*, House of Commons Library Briefing paper No. 7484, 24 November, updated using Source: https://data.oecd.org/inequality/income-inequality.htm, accessed March 2017.

respectively in 2009, are in the top seven in the Gini table in figure 1.3. Countries in which they take the least are in the bottom three: in Norway and Denmark they took 7% and 5% that same year. This is an enormous difference. Note that inequalities are only rising to new peaks in ten of the thirty-six countries included in figure 1.3. In most affluent countries in the world income inequalities are now below their recent peak heights.

Inequality matters, because 'Our lives don't make sense in abstraction, only when compared with the lives of others.'[10] Almost everyone grossly underestimates the extent of economic inequality. Furthermore, people in more unequal countries notoriously overestimate the likelihood of moving up the income scale and underestimate their chances of moving down.

Numeracy is on average far worse in more economically unequal countries, but that is not enough to explain the direction of bias in these misapprehensions. In the USA they have been put down to the power of the 'American Dream'; a dream that endures despite numerous reports of its demise.

Figure 1.4, which first appeared in the *New York Times* in December 2016, intimated that Americans going home to their parents that Christmas should be able to see that the dream was ending.[11]

Chance of making more money than your parents if you were...

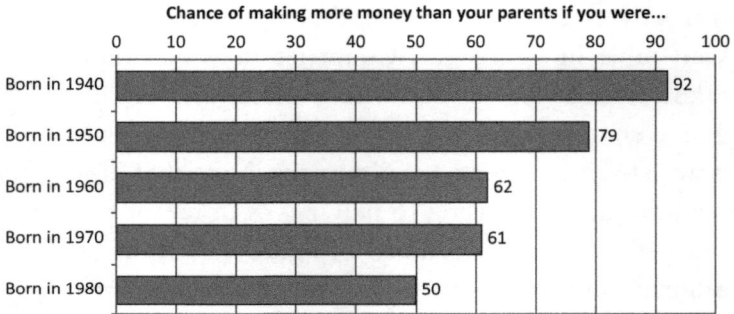

Figure 1.4 Being better off than your parents in the USA by decade by birth, chance (%)

Source: Leonhardt, D. (2016) The American Dream, quantified at last, *New York Times*, 8 December. Figure drawn from a subset of the data presented at http://www.equality-of-opportunity.org/ under the title 'The fading American Dream', accessed March 2017.

Despite it being far harder to escape poverty in the USA than in most of Europe, some 71% of Americans, as compared to 40% of Europeans, believe that the poor have a 'reasonable chance of escaping poverty'. A study published in 2015[12] found that poor Americans were much more likely to believe it was possible to move up the income scale than rich Americans believed it to be. The views of the rich were nearer to reality.

In the 2015 study, non-white participants were the most likely to believe upward mobility was likely. The study asked 3,034 Americans complex questions about probabilities in which they were reminded that their answers should sum to 100% to avoid them producing impossible estimates. But even when corrected for this their expectations were impossible.[13]

In 2013 President Obama said that misperceptions about inequality were a 'fundamental threat to the American Dream'.[14] Had he been braver he could have added that the dream itself was a chimera, reality was quite different. Only a few can ever get rich; it is a myth to believe that many can realize the dream because being rich *is* about having much more than almost everybody else.

The myth of the American Dream has been shown in the past to make Americans far less concerned about inequality, so it is little wonder they live with more inequality than most other folk in the rich world. A generation ago Americans who despised inequality were described as 'a sub-group of rich leftists'.[15] It was even claimed that they were suffering from 'inequality-generated unhappiness'! Today, far more Americans are unhappy with inequality. It was also better-off leftists who first highlighted rising inequality in the UK. As a result, government statisticians now more regularly report on its extent.

In London people live parallel lives according to their incomes. Almost all neighbourhoods in

Number of middle layer super output areas (average annual income)

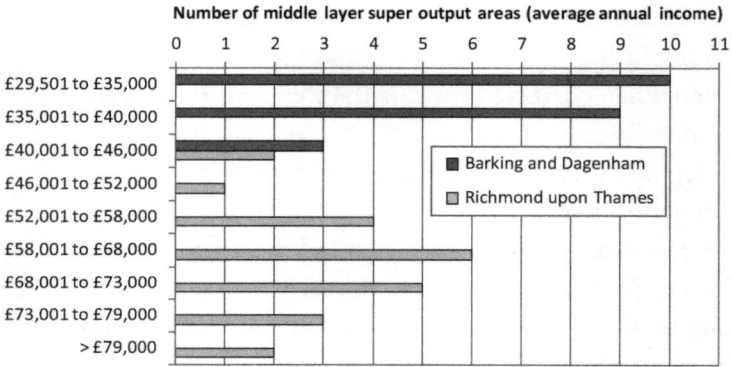

Figure 1.5 Distribution of household income in two London boroughs, 2013/2014

Source: ONS (2016) *Small Area Model-Based Income Estimates, England and Wales: financial year ending 2014*, London: ONS. The data this figure are based on are Crown Copyright (acknowledged).

London are now *more* mixed by ethnicity and religion than they were a decade ago, but *less* mixed by income.[16] Figure 1.5 shows the most recent estimates of average household income in different neighbourhoods for two London boroughs.[17] Everyone in Barking and Dagenham now lives in areas where mean household income is below £46,000 a year and in the majority of cases as low as around £30,000 a year. There is hardly any overlap with Richmond upon Thames on the opposite side of London. But within Richmond there are even greater disparities by neighbourhood.

Further away from London the majority of people (55%) in England and Wales live in neighbourhoods where average household incomes range between £17,000 and £39,000 a year.

It is important to note that not everything is getting worse in the UK. English schools were even more mixed ethnically in 2013 than in 2008. Research published in 2016 'shows that for all ethnic groups, segregation fell in far more places than it rose'.[18] Ethnic segregation fell the most for Pakistani students in those five years. British children are increasingly segregated by their parents' incomes, not by their race or religion.

The children of the affluent are most segregated through family money that allows them to have a home in a 'good area' or a place at a private school. Such a school place comes with many advantages, including being much more likely to be granted extra time in public examinations. Private schools register a fifth of their students as having a disability requiring special exam concessions, as compared to just one in eight state school students. This is not because more of the children of the rich are handicapped.[19] In 2016 it was revealed that '22% of young people from the richest fifth of the population get a place at one of the "top 40" universities, but only 2% of the poorest fifth'.[20] And children from the poorest fifth go almost entirely into the 'bottom' group of universities.

High income and wealth inequalities result in huge educational inequalities, but these could be mitigated. The inequalities we currently live with have not always been with us, they are a varying feature; they rise and fall. Worldwide they are today enormous. Within the USA, the UK, and especially London, they are stark. But they will change. Perpetually increasing inequality is unsustainable. Which is why inequalities so often fell in the past and are falling within most countries of the world today.[21]

2

A History of Inequality

I am Nigerian because the white man created Nigeria and gave me that identity. I am black because the white man constructed black to be as different as possible from white. But I was Igbo before the white man came.

Chimanamda Ngozi Adiche, 2007[1]

Inequality bequeathed modern day ethnicities. Our great modern rise in international inequality began with the Spanish and Portuguese invasion of the Americas. It was this collision of worlds, 'old' and 'new', which ushered in our current age of greatest-ever global inequality. That collision began a transition. Part way through the transition we gave it a name: 'capitalism'. To try to make sense of our times we saw them as more stable than they were. We saw them as an era, rather than a period of great change.

17

A transition that takes place over the course of many human lifetimes can look more like an *era* than a *change* to observers who each, individually, live and work and think and write for only a few dozen years. However, once most of that transformation has taken place the picture becomes clearer. As pointed out at the start of chapter 1, the Dutch were the first people in the modern era to begin to grow rich on trade. Figure 2.1 shows just how unequal things were in 1732 when the spoils of that trade were at first so unevenly distributed towards a few in Holland.

In contrast, colonial America was relatively egalitarian. Among all Americans the richest 1% took 8.5% of total income in 1774, just before their declaration of independence. Excluding slaves, the top 1% took 7.6%, very similar to Sweden today, whereas in the USA today the top 1% now take around 20% of all income despite slavery having been formally abolished.[2] The USA became more unequal as it became richer.

From at least 1914 onwards Holland and then the Netherlands as a whole became more equal as it became relatively poorer. Extreme inequality tends to be concentrated in those countries that are most effectively subjugated and those countries doing the majority of the subjugation. Among the three dominant countries shown in figure 2.1, inequalities

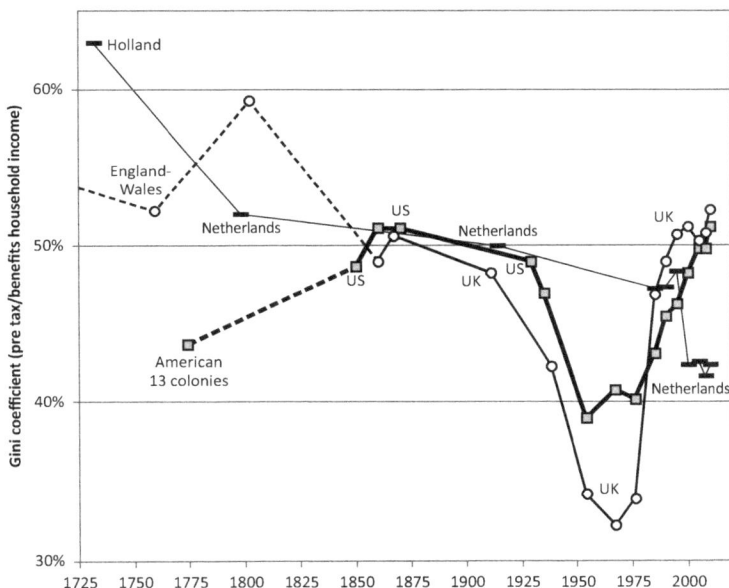

Figure 2.1 Income inequality in America, Britain and the Netherlands/Holland, 1732–2010

Source: Lindert, P. H. and Williamson, J. G. (2016) *Unequal Gains: American growth and inequality since 1700*, Princeton: Princeton University Press, figure 5.4. Reproduced with permission from Peter Lindert, http://voxeu.org/article/american-growth-and-inequality-1700. Note the UK is more unequal than the USA prior to tax and welfare redistribution.

fell the most in the UK during the 1960s when there was the greatest fall in income from its colonies, and before the most recent expansion of inequality began. They are lowest in the Netherlands now, perhaps as its people have mostly abandoned an imperial mind-set?

The American colonies were an exception. They were less exploited than other colonies. Inequalities rose greatly in the world following colonization including within the countries that exploited colonies. Before then there had *not* been huge global differences in annual incomes and total wealth. But after the colonies were first created and capitalism was spread worldwide in the seventeenth and eighteenth centuries, a perpetual wealth-inequality-creating machine appeared to have been set in motion.

Consider another graph. Figure 2.2 shows GDP per person trends in twelve regions of the world since 1820 relative to the mean average world GDP per capita. It suggests that the capitalist ever-increasing-inequality-machine did not function as reliably as had often been assumed and is certainly faltering today, capitalism is itself still transforming as global inequalities start to fall.

Figure 2.2 reveals that by 1820 North America was becoming richer and Europe had pulled even further ahead of the rest of the world. By 1939 European incomes then rose to 2.5 times the world average and North American incomes were touching 5.0 times shortly afterwards! The world was

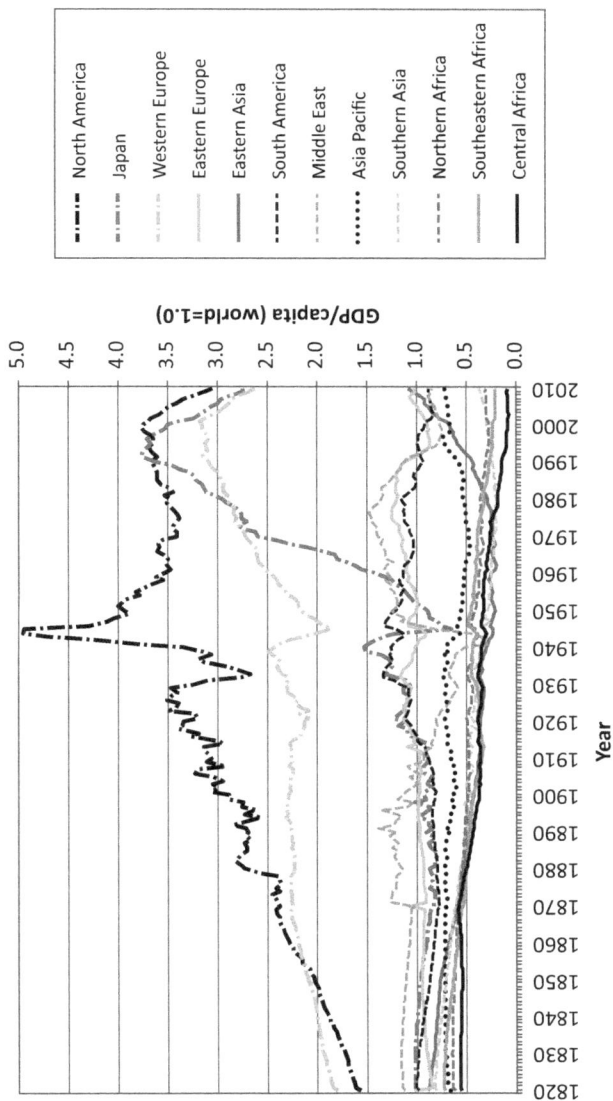

Figure 2.2 GDP per capita using Worldmapper world region 1820–2010, relative scale

Source: www.worldmapper.org updated by Bolt, J. and van Zanden, J. L. (2014) The Maddison Project: collaborative research on historical national accounts, *The Economic History Review*, 67, 3, pp. 627–51.

21

extremely unequal when World War II began. A few decades later North American dominance waned as Western Europe began to recover and Japan shot up, but global inequalities did not fall until just after the millennium.

Europe originally became richer on the back of colonization through exploitation ranging from slavery, through indenture, to installing and maintaining deplorable pay and conditions and the imposition of unfair terms of trade. When the USA became hegemonic it followed suit. It had few formal colonies but it was involved in colonial wars, from Korea to Vietnam. US officials tried to hide their involvement in many other wars.

The hiding of history matters because it is through 'collective remembering' that people 'orientate social movements towards imagining, and creating, a future more congruent with their desires'.[3] In the fifteenth century, when the Portuguese and Spanish landed on the coast of what is now Nigeria, they came at first to trade. When the British came it was to take power. The present day inequality between Nigeria and Britain is due to the initial and subsequent exercising of that power. We too easily forget this history when considering current inequality.

'The struggle of man against power is the struggle of memory against forgetting.'[4] This is often reworded now to say 'people' instead of 'man',[5] but doing that itself hides a huge part of how we came to see women as so inferior. That we worry about such things now, the use of the word 'man', and the fact that we are now uncovering so many not completely concealed secrets, all point towards how we now see the world so very differently than we did just a generation ago. As the transition slows, our ability to see ourselves more clearly accelerates; we begin to see old information in a new light.

Figure 2.3 compares the changes between 1950 and 2010 in average per capita GDP in Nigeria and the UK, the places where some people had previously been called Igbo and others Britons. Without the ratio being shown it would be impossible to appreciate the changes that have happened over such a short time.

Nigeria (per person) has veered between being almost 7.5 times and 17.5 times less well-off than the UK in just the course of one recent short human lifetime (60 years). The ratio shows a huge relative gap between the two countries but nothing is set in stone about what the size of that gap need be and hence what it might be in future. Inequalities are not stable, both within and between countries.

A great deal of the detail of how rising economic inequality was achieved has been destroyed.

Ratio of GDP/capita shown as a thick line and scale on left hand axis

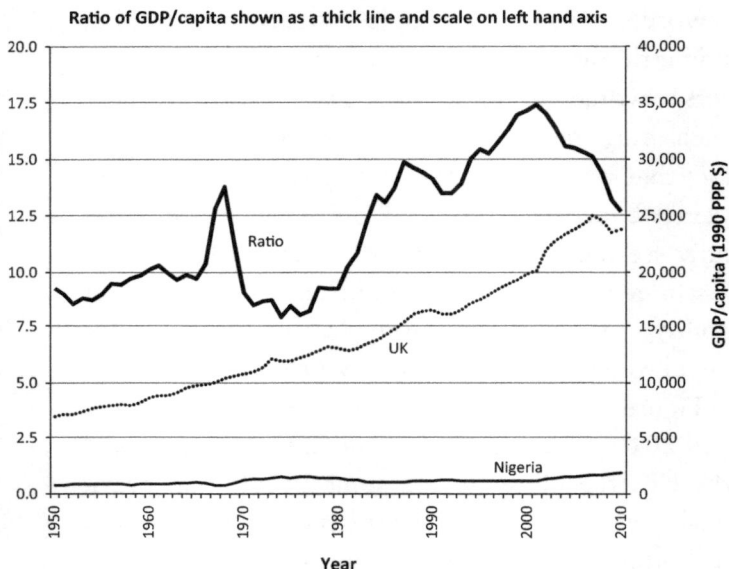

Figure 2.3 GDP per capita, comparison, Nigeria and the UK, 1950–2010

Source: Calculated by author from www.worldmapper.org updated by Bolt, J. and van Zanden, J. L. (2014) The Maddison Project: collaborative research on historical national accounts, *The Economic History Review*, 67, 3, pp. 627–51.

'Operation Legacy'[6] was the name given in the 1950s and 1960s to the destruction and concealment of official archives that might have embarrassed or compromised the British, or could be interpreted as evidence of extreme racism warranting prosecution and reparations. Long before people in Nigeria were 'given' independence in 1963, those archives detailed how and why they came to receive each year ten times less per person than the Britons.

Other sources have been hidden and marked top secret: 'By the time the greatest of Empires was finally being dissolved, the most important consideration for those in government, in Whitehall and the colonies, was that the British way of doing things should be recalled with fondness and respect and the retreat should be recorded as a dignified affair.'[7] Ian Cobain, the journalist who came to this conclusion, did so when he found that some 20,000 documents were retained as a 'migrated archive', marked to be handled only by those of European descent. It is impossible to defend current worldwide economic inequality without also being racist.

The migrated archive is held at Hanslope Park[8] in Buckinghamshire. It still contains documents which demonstrate that in another former British colony, Kenya, 'the torture and murder had been systemic – choreographed, in fact, by colonial administrators and the colony's law officers – ministers and officials in London had been fully aware of the details of the abuses . . . abuses that the British public had repeatedly been assured throughout the 1950s were not happening'.[9]

Instructions were left that all papers should be destroyed that showed 'religious intolerance on the part of Her Majesty's Government and all papers which might be interpreted as showing racial discrimination against Africans (or Negroes in the USA)'.[10] But as so much was changing so quickly they failed to destroy all the papers.

Clearly the British officials who gave these orders were worried that they might have to face a court case before they were dead. They may also have sensed that a great alteration was underway, a change to the nature of the capitalist transformation. Indeed, enormous social change *was* taking place in Britain in the 1960s, followed by economic turmoil in the 1970s that was part of a global economic crisis that decade, which in turn led to further crises.

At the end of the 1970s an economic crash occurred in the Middle East, quickly followed by the Iranian revolution of 1979. That year average GDP per capita of the Middle East as a whole came within a fraction of 1.5 times the global average. It fell from then onwards. Eastern Europe saw incomes fall rapidly from just before 1989, when the Berlin Wall was breached. Figure 2.2 shows that relative incomes next began to fall in Japan, following the great Tokyo housing crash of the early 1990s.

A History of Inequality

Shortly before the millennium incomes fell in South America during the great Argentinian depression, which followed the Brazilian crisis.[11] That in turn followed the Asian financial crisis, and was all followed by the European crisis. Relative incomes fell in North America from 2001 and especially rapidly after 2008. In recent years incomes have been static in Africa, have risen slightly in South Asia and have only risen continuously in East Asia.

The current rise of China and the relative fall of the rest is part of a transition from a world of great regional *equality* to one of wide geographical *inequalities* and now the beginning of a return towards what was seen before 1820 – when there were narrower differences. But the poorest parts of Africa have yet to see any turnaround. South Asia (mostly India) has leap-frogged Africa after more than half a century of independence from Britain. China, which was the poorest region in the 1950s, is now the fourth best-off region. Most recently, all the three richest regions began dipping down, as figure 2.2 makes very clear. The very near future may be more equitable.

The history of inequality is a large part of the history of humanity. Of all the twelve regions shown in figure 2.2, Japan had some of the highest rates of economic *inequality* prior to World War II. In contrast, the USA was one of the most equitable of nations just two centuries ago and again just fifty years ago. Europe is full of contrasts, with the UK having been the second most equitable large European nation in the 1970s and now being the most unequal.

The point being repeatedly made here is that rates of inequality fluctuate. High rates are rarely sustained for long and tend to lead to disaster, such as instigating and losing a war, or suffering a stock market crash. In contrast, economic inequalities tend to rise slowly, rather than abruptly. Stepping back is the only way to see all this; figure 2.2 is of seven human generations of change, figure 2.3 encompasses just one lifetime. The change within any one human lifetime is not understandable other than as part of a larger pattern. Figure 2.1 took an even longer view.

Figures 2.1, 2.2 and 2.3 partly explain how notions of racial superiority arise. In the 1970s researchers[12] joked of undertaking a project that involved enslaving a group of whites from the US and UK, taking them to West Africa and, 200 years later, after giving them a minimal education, testing their descendants on IQ tests standard-ized on black children. The whites would appear inferior.

We have only recently come to realize that Europeans were simply the people who happened to be living furthest West on the Eurasian island, next to those ocean currents that most easily propel a ship to the Americas. It was only long after that ocean crossing that the Igbo would be called Nigerians. Nigeria was not even defined as a British protectorate until 1901.

Although GDP per capita inequalities are now falling between world regions, the many earlier decades of rising income inequalities led to huge worldwide wealth inequalities, as well as an enormous legacy of racism and an ignorance of our collective history. We are now waking up; hence so many current calls to de-colonialize the curriculum in universities. We are also wising up to being robbed by the wealthiest of all. Between the years 2000 and 2015 in the UK the wealthiest 1% of the population saw their wealth rise by £1,500,000 (on average), whereas the poorest 10% of people saw their average wealth increase by only £500 each, or by three thousand times less![13]

Today the best-off 1% in the UK is at risk of viewing the bottom 10% like the colonialists viewed the natives and the slaves. They use new names to describe people beneath them: 'troubled families', 'the underclasses', and older names too, such as 'beggars' and 'trash'.[14] We have been here before. As some historians lament: 'This all seems to have been thoroughly forgotten. Modern welfare states since

1945 have been seen as something completely new. This amnesia is perhaps due to the radical reforms of the Poor Laws in 1834. These reforms dramatically altered their character from a universal system to one based on utilitarianism. The 1834 "New" Poor Laws were premised on ideas of individual self-interest, choice, and responsibility.'[15] Inequalities remained very high in the UK up until the point when those Poor Laws were watered down after World War I and, in effect, repealed after World War II.

The geographical variation in *choices* affecting inequality is also often forgotten. The UK pursued policies to increase inequality after 1979 in a way that both set it apart from the rest of Europe and which has been shown to have devastated whole cities.[16] As Britain's hold over its former colonies weakened and as its importance to North America diminished, port cities on its western seaboard suffered especially.

Glasgow and Liverpool prospered when ships brought cotton and other goods from the Americas then travelled down to Africa with merchandise and back to the Americas with Igbo and other cargo. Long after the slave trade ended they continued to prosper from other less overtly unfair trade. It was not until most of the trade ended that the cities shrank. The ports nearer to the European mainland faired better. Old wharfs on the Thames were turned into gleaming citadels to trade money.

Inequalities influence politics, policies and perceptions. In the immediate aftermath of the UK Brexit vote, the London banks, led by 'Bank of America Merrill Lynch', began to warn their most wealthy customers that 'Brexit is thus far the biggest electoral riposte yet to our age of inequality'. Meanwhile a UK fund manger advised companies to pay an equitable rate of tax, stating that: 'not paying taxes damages the brand'.[17]

In a considered response to the earlier 2008 banking crisis researchers studying the largest US and UK banks concluded that 'banking should be treated as a public good or a public utility'[18] and that these changes should be implemented in the immediate aftermath of the next financial crisis which, when they were writing in 2016, was seen likely to be coming within the next few years.

At the start of 2017, following the Trump and Brexit votes, many of the world's richest business leaders who meet each year at Davos declared the rise of inequality as the greatest threat of all, and suggested that a fundamental change was required in capitalism. They concluded that boosting growth alone would not remedy the deeper fractures in our political economy.

The world's business elite declared that root and branch reforms to market capitalism were needed to tackle the lack of solidarity between those at the top and those further down. But apart from recognizing the greater need for long-term thinking regarding capitalism, all they could come up with was: 'recognition of the importance of identity and inclusiveness in political communities; mitigating the risks and exploiting the opportunities of new technologies such as driverless cars; and strengthening global cooperation'.[19]

Change may be underway, despite the lacklustre enthusiasm of world business leaders. Since 1995 there has been little evidence of a *general* increase in income inequality within countries. According to the Peterson Institute for International Economics, within about half of all countries for which they had measures, inequality fell compared to the third that have seen them rise. In the remaining countries there was no recorded change. At exactly the same time, most inequalities between countries have also been falling.[20] The 2015 study this finding comes from suggested that such falls will continue. That political action will now be taken to make them fall further, or at the very least halt them from rising.

3

Why Argue for Inequality?

I know a lot of people that have second homes in
London and I'm so glad they do. Even if they're here
only for a few weeks and throw some key parties,
these are amazing multiplying events.

Patrik Schumacher, architect,
November 2016[1]

Traditionally, tolerance of inequality has been
couched in terms of it encouraging economic
growth, trickle-down, aspirations and social mobility, creativity, competition and innovation. Today
few people make such arguments because the evidence for each one can now be seen to be so weak.
For instance, the 'marginal revenue productivity
theory of wages' suggests that market forces ensure
that people *are only paid* what they are worth. This
is clearly nonsense. At numerous points in this very
short book all these 'justifications' are refuted.

Why Argue for Inequality?

Advocates of greater inequality are not numerous, but they tend to be rich, or financially backed by the rich. In 2016, at the World Architecture Festival in Berlin, Patrik Schumacher, director of Zaha Hadid architects, made the headlines when he argued that ownership of little-used second homes by the very wealthy in London was a great thing because of the multiplier effects that arose from the parties they might throw.

Schumacher's argument, when looked at a little more closely, was basically that what makes money is good. All other considerations appeared to be irrelevant. In the speech that the above quote was taken from, he also listed eight specific demands, every one of which would increase inequality. These included planners being prevented from doing little more than ensuring safe access to private property and the right to light.

Schumacher suggested that only 'the market' should decide what land should be used for. Hyde Park could be built over. There should be no housing standards, no minimum required floor area for homes depending on the numbers of bedrooms, and no social or affordable housing should be provided. All other government interventions should be removed, including regulation of tenancies. And, finally, he called for the privatization of streets, squares, public spaces and parks, even entire urban districts.

Schumacher may be an extreme example of an inequality advocate, someone who believes that the state should be getting out of the way of the free market, but he is also an example of someone who voices what other very wealthy people think, but *do not say publicly*. He makes vocal the reason why the elite of cities like London allow so many homes in its centre to be empty for much of the year. Many of them have come to believe that 'the market' is the best decision maker. There is now overwhelming evidence that it is not.

The argument that markets know best has only been vigorously made within living memory and it was made at a point when uncertainty was great-est. In *The Road to Serfdom*, written during World War II, Friedrich August von Hayek argued that a concern with greater equality through central plan-ning and regulation creates an oppressive society, the tyranny of a dictator, followed by individual servitude. Hayek thought that only free markets improved the general level of wealth. When he was writing both Stalin and Hitler were in power.

Hayek argued that markets set prices better than committees, that someone is worth what the market will pay them, and that free enterprise left unfettered always produces the best results. His arguments were later taken up by some of those who became rich, as a vindication that their riches were *appropriately* earned. For them it would be wrong and inefficient to limit any single individual's ability to amass wealth, as that would reduce *market efficiency*. For them the market was an all-knowing mechanism that could determine the true value of anything and thus fairly reward those who really are worth more.

In practice the market, when not well regulated, rewards those the most who are the most greedy and unscrupulous, which then results in greater inefficiency; hence the lower rates of economic growth seen in the USA and UK in recent decades. The greedy are not 'the best'. The most unscrupulous of all lobby government vigorously to reduce regulations, which is why fossil fuel magnates, unhealthy food conglomerates and tobacco companies spend so much setting up think tanks that they pretend not to fund, including those think tanks in the 1970s that spread Hayek's philosophy.

In the UK in the 1980s Margaret Thatcher was a follower of Hayek. She grew up when the UK was becoming less rich in comparison to other European nations and those around her blamed this on UK politics promoting greater equality rather than the consequence of the unavoidable loss of empire. Figure 3.1 shows the trends over 115 years in five rich states to illustrate just how variable inequality trends have been in different countries at different times.

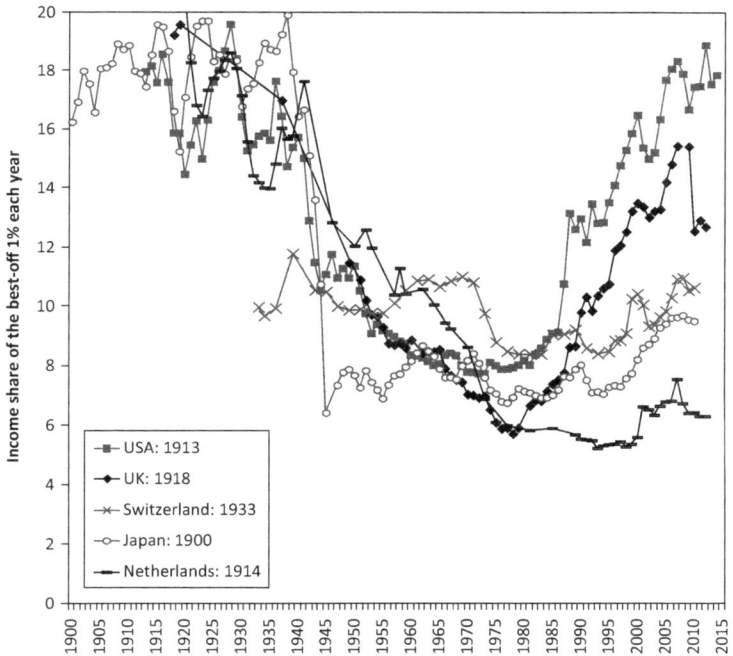

Figure 3.1 Take of the 1% in five affluent nations, 1900–2010

Source: World Wealth and Income Dataset, http://wid.world/, accessed January 2017.
Note: the year each dataset begins is given in the legend.

Why Argue for Inequality?

In those countries where politicians more often became advocates of free market economics, those who grew richest profited by hidden and not so hidden state interventions and state support on their behalf. They did not actually believe in a completely free market, they believed in a 'free market' propped up by a state that serves their and their friends' interests.

Four of these five countries were similarly inequitable before World War II. The one exception was Switzerland. It was more equal than the others, stayed out of the war and then became the most unequal in the 1960s and 1970s before inequalities were also reduced there. It is now the average country of these five, with its best-off 1% now taking about 10.5% of all Swiss income each year.

In contrast Japan, which was the most unequal of all the five countries before the war, became the most equal after it, and is still the second most equitable. Great equality emerged in Japan as the rich lost most of their rentier (by rent) incomes when the invading American forces took their estates away and redistributed the land. At first no one was better off, but then average Japanese incomes rose and rose, as shown figure 2.2.

The country that did become the most equal of all these five was the Netherlands. Recall (figure 2.1) that by around 1732 the lands that now have that name contained the richest and most unequal provinces in the world. Three centuries later it had become one of the most equitable places in the world. Not surprisingly inequality fell in the Netherlands after both World Wars, but *significantly* it was not allowed to subsequently rise. The Netherlands is a place that has learnt better than most how to curb greed.

The USA is the state among these five in which inequalities have been allowed to grow the greatest, since reaching a minimum in the 1950s when, for a brief few years, the USA was the most equitable of all five countries shown in the figure. However, the USA was also the country that was the richest in 1950 and, when its riches diminished in relative terms, compared to the world average, it then adapted least well.

On losing its top spot, the USA allowed those already with most to begin to take even more at the expense of the poorest 99% of its own society. And the USA continues to be home to those who fund think tanks that promote inequality the most. The 2016 meeting of the Mont Pèrelin Society,[2] which was held in the USA, included a paper arguing that women were paid less just because they were worth less.[3]

Finally, the UK can be seen to have followed the USA, although not yet to such great extremes of inequality. However, it has still reached the greatest extreme in Europe (see figure 1.3), and it is currently uncertain where it is going. The apparent fall in the graph in figure 3.1 for the UK recently could be real, or due to increased tax avoidance, aided by accountants.[4] But if you thought that rising income inequality was a sign of market efficiency then you would not see the rise in inequality as problematic at all. For you it would simply be an indication that the market had become less fettered and was now rewarding those who should be rewarded more.

Markets are not made more efficient when there is more competition, because the firms that become bigger, by chance, will only continue to do well in an unregulated system if they spend money ensuring their rivals cannot rise or gain a competitive advantage. The winners more often engage in illegal activity, which is so much easier with less regulation around. Oligarchy increases, including the control of the press. As competition expert Will Davies explains: 'it's as if the top football team has bought not only the best coaches, physios and facilities, but also bought the referee and the journalists as well'.[5]

It is worth repeating that the UK had become the second most equitable large European country by the 1970s. It had also become less affluent in relation to other European countries. In hindsight the two trends do *not* appear to be connected; the UK became poorer as it lost its empire. However, as so many people in the UK had never accepted that exploiting the empire was a major reason for its wealth then, when those riches went, initially the trade unions at home were blamed.

The trade unions were followed by other scapegoats – the unemployed, benefit scroungers, EU regulations and immigrants. Then utilities from water to trains were privatized, creating even more huge expensive inefficiencies.

Many British industries and services had developed around the existence of the colonies. It was not only that income and wealth from the colonies stopped pouring in, but also that losing them left the country with an inefficient industrial infrastructure that could not adjust quickly. The USA similarly, but a little later, found it hard to adjust to no longer dominating other countries through military and commercial might in the 1980s and 1990s.

Advocates of inequality argue for 'Empire 2.0' (re-establishing former colonial relationships) and often more military spending. They often do not realize that many in China and India now hold the country that once oppressed them in low esteem.[6]

The political right often have a very skewed view of history; they could not be on the right without it.

The administration of Ronald Reagan, who presided over a period of rapidly increasing economic inequality, was viewed as a wonderful development by many on the right – both at the time and subsequently. Copying Thatcher in the UK, Reagan made arguments for 'letting tall poppies grow'. When understood in the geographical and historical context of the time it is possible to see how such arguments could have been convincingly made. With hindsight they were clearly fallacious.[7]

Neither in the USA nor in the UK did the mysterious trickle-down effect operate, whereby the poor became better off as a consequence of the rich first becoming better off. The poorer half of all adults in the USA received 1% less in real terms in 2015 as compared to 1978. In contrast, in France, with redistributive 'trickle-up', the incomes of the poorest half rose by 39% over the same time period.[8]

One justification made for inequality being a good thing is that its existence incentivizes and motivates people to produce wealth. These people have often been called the 'wealth creators', and the story that is told tends to follow the line that if people starting off in business did not think they could become extremely rich then they would not start. The problem with the argument is that many people in very equitable countries start new businesses and their business usually performs better and fails less often. Thus not as many new businesses are needed to replace them as in unequal countries. However, inequality advocates welcome business failure as 'creative destruction'. For them there is never a reason not to support high and rising inequality.

Advocates of inequality often resort to using 'freedom' as their argument of last resort. However, relatively low levels of inequality are compatible with a very high level of personal freedom. Being properly taxed is not an excessive or unreasonable restriction on personal freedom. More useful wealth is created in countries with greater economic equality, which have workforces that are more productive and which delay gratification rather than prioritize the immediate profit and consumption motive.

Some say that measures to tackle inequality can be counterproductive, in that the wealthy can move their wealth abroad, rendering the tackling of inequality fruitless. Again those arguments could have held some credibility in the 1970s before they were tested, but having tested them we find that wealth does not flee the world's most equitable countries such as Norway, the Netherlands or Germany. Today an enormous amount of business in the UK and USA is actually owned by companies based abroad, companies that are headquartered in more equitable nations; much of the UK rail network is now run by such companies while the people who profit from running those companies live in countries with efficient nationalized rail systems!

Another argument for inequality is that it increases equality of opportunity, if not outcomes, because, despite there being more opportunities to fail in a more unequal society, there are a few more opportunities to become exceedingly rich. Economic anthropologist Susana Narotzky has looked at such claims and concluded that inequality of opportunity, having less of a chance, is itself an outcome of tolerating basic economic inequalities.[9]

Often the advocates of inequality appear perplexed that they need to defend inequality at all, especially if they are neoclassical economists.[10] As the economist Branko Milanovic succinctly explains: 'Let's start from the beginning – why the neoclassical theory did not, and still does not study economic inequality. The reasons are very clear: inequality simply stems from the assumptions of the economic model, hence it does not need further research.'[11]

Why Argue for Inequality?

But why in the UK and USA, why in these countries and not in others, was the most rapid recent rise in inequality tolerated, supported and encouraged? Perhaps those who had great wealth here in the past had a greater sense of a lost entitlement than the rich elsewhere? That sense of loss led to arguments for inequality being particularly ferocious in those countries and evidence for the existence of *inherent equality* being more often ignored there.[12]

There have always been people who have tried to justify the inequalities of their times by claiming inherent differences. And arguments supporting these divisions have been of their time, and not surprisingly in the twentieth century they were often presented as 'scientific'.

In the twentieth century identical and non-identical twins were seen as a natural experiment to disentangle nature from nurture – the contributions of genetics and the environment. Advocates of inequality use twin studies to claim that most of the differences between children's various academic abilities are due to genetic make-up. All this then supports the concept of providing the children of the usually financially better off with better educational facilities that results in them, in turn, often becoming financially better off.

However, in 2013 a paper was published that uncovered what may be very important new evidence.[13] It also studied twins, but included ones who were brought up assuming they were identical, but later (genetically) found not to be (they were dizygotic or DZ), and the opposite, twins thought to be not identical, but who technically were (they were monozygotic or MZ).

Those incorrectly thought to be identical started with very similar birth weights and ended with very similar heights and weights. What was interesting was that the assessment of their academic ability, using the cumulative high school grade point average, was equally as highly correlated as that for twins correctly thought to be identical.

What twin studies often actually reveal is that similarly looking children have similar outcomes in life, especially if they are born at the same time and place (as all twins are). They do not reveal that some people are genetically superior to others in overall ability. Rather that we live in societies that have strong prejudices over how people are treated based simply on looks and first impressions.

This paper was the first because, as its authors said, 'we are the first to apply the misclassified twins approach to a recent sample with accurate genetic zygosity information for all twins'.[14] What was found should cause us to doubt many of the conclusions drawn from older twin studies by advocates of inherent genetic inequalities in, for example, academic ability.

It is researchers based in the USA or UK who have undertaken most studies that claim genetic differences between groups are very important. These extremely unequal countries are odd in many other ways. They are also home to most of the strongest advocates for greater inequality in the world. They are also odd in that the USA and UK are now *the two most* significant arms dealing states in the world with the UK government alone having licensed arms exports to 22 of the 30 countries on its own human rights watch list since 2010! Elites in more unequal countries encourage less moral behaviour.

The UK and USA provide a more comfortable home for inequality advocates than any other affluent countries. They are places where advocacy of inequality can be fostered and feel normal.[15] One inequality advocate proclaimed that 'the majority of those who are born poor swiftly move up the income ladder, and almost all become wealthier than their parents'.[16] We can look at figure 1.4 to see that this is not true.

There are many more arguments for inequality; for instance that it helps support the arts and higher things in life. Whether that argument works for you depends on what you make of the art being funded. Writer Amber A'Lee Frost found that 'today's "patrons of the arts" are less interested in opera and ballet, and more interested in novelty furniture and enormous sculptures of their own faces'.[17] The novel furniture isn't even useful, it includes chairs you cannot sit on. As she says: 'I cannot stress this enough; it's just terrible, ugly fucking furniture.' It is very hard to argue for inequality when you see much of what the rich actually squander their money on, including useless and ugly chairs that each cost enough to feed an entire village in a poor country for many years!

One reason to argue for inequality is that someone is paying you to do it, such as a think tank funded by a rich donor or a newspaper owned by a very rich man; people desperately seeking to justify the riches they hold. The advocates of inequality tend to be driven either by self-interested rich people or the paid toadies of the rich. As Thomas Hobbes put it in 1651: 'the difference between man and man is not so considerable'.[18]

4

Who Benefits
from Inequality?

The life expectancy at 40 years of age in the top
income percentile of the United States is better than
the mean in any other country for life expectancy at
40 years of age. However, not by a lot, and likely
not better than the top percentile in Sweden or the
Netherlands. In contrast, the life expectancy at 40
years of age in the bottom income percentile of
the United States is located between the mean for
Pakistan and Sudan for life expectancy at 40 years
of age.

Angus Deaton, 2016[1]

It sounds like a stupid question. Clearly it is the very
richest 1% who benefit from inequality. But how
much do they really benefit? Before considering the
quality of their lives, the quote above would suggest by just a few extra months of life on average.
Compared to the worst off in their own country

the best-off 1% of US men live 15 years longer. For women that gap is 10 years. Those who are just below the 1% see much less apparent benefit.[2] But there is much more to living a good life than living a longer life.

Think about just being able to go for a walk, not thinking that you need to be driven past neighbourhoods that you would never dream of walking through. Think about going shopping or to a park. Could you just go, or would you have to be very careful about where you went, and when you went? Even the very wealthy, in an unequal country, need to think whether it is safe around where they live in the evening.

It is rarely realized that when inequality is high the very best off also suffer from greater inequality. Just within the best-off tenth of the population in a very unequal country there are always huge financial inequalities. Most people within the top 10% will not feel that they are doing particularly well. In fact even within the top 1% there will be many individuals who think they do not have enough to keep up with those around them.

Consider Brazil. The latest data, which are for 2013, show that the best-off 10% of people who live there take 51% of the total personal income in that country. However, within that top 10% it is their best-off tenth ('the 1%') who take by far the most – 23% of all income, leaving those in the rest of the top tenth with much less; as badly treated by the top 1% as the 90% are treated by the top 10%. But it doesn't stop there. As Table 4.1 shows, the best-off 0.1% get 44% of the top 1%'s take, most of the '1%' are thus getting around 50 times average Brazilian earnings which leaves the '0.01%' receiving 500 times average earning, each!

Getting by on 50 times what most people have to live on might sound like luxury, but it is not 'most people' that the 1% mix with. When they mix with those just above them, they can feel poor, and when they mix with those just beneath them, they can view them as poor (even though they are not). Then there is all the expense of being that well off: spending on security, on living in a safe area, on a suitably grand, often bullet-proof, car; on 'top-grade' (private) education; and on trying to keep up appearances to look reputable in front of those they need to impress.

Great inequality is precarious. There was a doubling of the wealth of the Brazilian 0.01% in just the two years from 2006 to 2008 (see table 4.1). That group had large investments in assets that suddenly became more valuable because of the financial

Who Benefits from Inequality?

Table 4.1 Share of annual income in Brazil received by those at the top (%)

	0.01%	0.10%	1%	10%
1926	3.8	10.3	20.0	-
1936	3.5	10.0	22.4	-
1946	4.4	12.5	28.2	-
1956	2.6	8.4	22.2	-
1966	2.4	7.6	21.7	-
1976	2.4	7.7	23.6	60.2
1986	8.0	13.3	24.8	50.5
1996	4.6	10.1	22.1	52.4
...				
2006	3.7	9.0	21.7	49.5
2007	5.0	9.8	21.3	47.1
2008	6.2	11.6	24.9	53.3
2009	5.0	10.0	22.8	50.6
2010	5.3	10.3	22.9	50.2
2011	5.9	11.1	23.7	50.4
2012	5.2	10.4	23.2	51.5
2013	4.9	10.1	22.9	51.5

Source: Pedro Herculano Guimarães Ferreira de Souza (personal communication, December 2016).

crisis. They owned gold, or in a very few cases even gold mines, and held much of their money in foreign currency. Those just below them lost out. People belonging to groups of similar wealth and status tend to diversify their wealth in very similar ways as they use the same wealth advisers.

Who Benefits from Inequality?

Brazil is one of the most economically *unequal* countries in the world today. Table 4.1 shows how these inequalities at the very top appear to have been falling ever so slightly since 2008. Before then the distribution of incomes within the top 10% shifted around, exacerbating the financial anxieties of people within this very affluent group.

All these numbers and proportions are confusing and dehumanizing. If they were not, if we had a natural affinity with the mathematics of inequality, then we would never have allowed inequalities to have risen as they have and to be as high as they are. No one defends the top tenth of Brazilians taking half the income of that country each year. No one says this is sane.

Somewhere is always the most unequal. Worldwide at the moment it is probably Brazil, although it competes for top place with South Africa.[3] Unusually for any country, it has for at least a century seen its top 1% take at least 20% of all income, but that does not mean it will always be so unequal. In October 2016 *Forbes Magazine* was celebrating the failure of the Brazilian Workers' Party to win control in the local elections, but it noted that no other politicians were popular either. This American business magazine advises on finance and investment, including investing in Brazil.[4]

The Brazilian investments that are of interest to those with money living outside Brazil are natural resources and, above all, oil. Countries with reserves of oil, or diamonds, or anything seen as being of great financial worth at any particular time tend to suffer from high inequalities. As *The Economist* explained to its readers over a decade ago: 'oil-rich countries do far less to help the poor than do countries without resources'.[5] But *The Economist* did not come up with a convincing reason as to why, and it did not mention the effects of those offshore 'investors'.

The very wealthy from one unequal country can have spillover effects into another, when they can exploit an easy source of profit. The effect of this exploitation is to concentrate the remaining profit after the foreign investors have taken their slice. Those who manage the extractive industries and the finance sectors that support them take as much as they can get away with. Some of this profit is then passed down to their own children.

In May 2016 Miles Corak updated his increasingly well-known international estimates of intergenerational social mobility.[6] The elasticity measure he uses is closely related to the correlation between parents' and their adult children's income. The results (see figure 4.1) suggested that China had the second

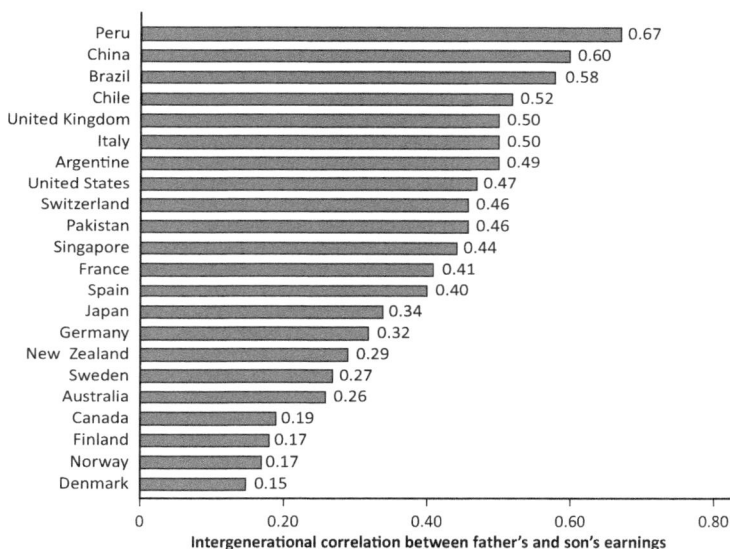

Figure 4.1 Intergenerational social mobility in selected countries, 2016

Source: Corak, M. (2016) *Inequality from Generation to Generation, the United States in Comparison*, IZA Discussion Paper 9929, May, http:// ftp.iza.org/dp9929.pdf. Reproduced with permission from Miles Corak.

lowest social mobility of all the countries compared because of the huge differences between rural and urban incomes in China. Above China was Peru, and just below it Brazil. In contrast, in Denmark, in Norway, in Finland and in Canada your parents' background has the least influence on your own future.[7] Two of those countries, Norway and

Canada, exploit large deposits of oil and tar sands, but they don't allow foreign investors to control those industries, especially Norway, which as a consequence is much more equitable than Canada.

Social mobility inversely correlates with economic inequality. Your parents' economic background least influences your own in the Scandinavian countries, and in Japan, Germany and Canada. There it matters far less to whom you are born. In contrast, in the UK even if you make it from the working class into the middle class you will, on average, be paid £6,800 (17%) less a year than your colleagues who had middle class backgrounds and so 'look the part'. Mobility in one generation is a chimera in the most inequitable countries.[8]

So who benefits from the great inequality in countries that are more economically unequal? Is it the children of the very well off who can also expect to be well off? Not really as they are only *more likely* to be well off. They are *not certain* to be. The 'elasticity coefficient' of 0.58 for Brazil in figure 4.1 does not imply certainty, just a greater *chance* of being as rich or as poor as their parents. For the extremely rich their children's fortunes depend on how their overseas investments fare.

What would you prefer? To live in Norway and almost certainly be OK, even if you drop down, as the drop is not far; or to be born in a richer family in Brazil and have a lower chance of dropping down, but a more drastic drop if you do? And who would you trust?

There are huge variations in the World Value Survey answers to the following question: 'In general, do you think that most people can be trusted, or, alternatively that you can't be too careful in dealing with people?' As many as 64% of people in Norway say others can be trusted as compared to *only* 5% in Brazil. This is directly related to both the greater equality in Norway and the greater happiness to be found there. Economists now routinely find that: 'The most satisfied countries are generally those in Scandinavia, as well as the Netherlands and Switzerland.'[9]

If you are not yet convinced that very few people benefit from greater inequality think of what job choices you have in a more unequal country if you wish to be in the best-off 10% or 1%. The university I teach in channels a disproportionate number of its students into careers in finance in London, not because they studied subjects to do with finance at university, but because that is where the highest pay is. To young adults it seems more crucial, safer (in an unequal country like the UK) to try to secure a highly paid job. But then in most cases those who secure these jobs then work absurdly long hours and end up doing banking jobs that they often find boring and soul-destroying.

The financial sector of a country tends to grow when inequalities grow, but people within that sector are never presented as a happy bunch. In the UK there are 586,000 people who are accountants of one kind or another. This is more than in all the rest of Europe combined. In France and Germany the number of accountants is around 34,000 each.[10] Accountancy appears to be not needed so much in those more equitable European countries, perhaps because people there don't try so hard to avoid paying their taxes? Accountancy is not a dream job unless what you dream about is money.

In the USA the proportions and numbers of lawyers working in business are reported to be even more ridiculous than the number of accountants in Britain. Around the year 1980 there were 450,000 lawyers working in the USA and that was seen as highly excessive then, but by 2011 the total had risen to 1.22 million. The rate of increase has slowed a little since, but lawyers are still an increasing proportion of the US population.[11]

Lawyers don't make anything. They don't teach children, they don't heal the sick, but they do sort out legal messes, including divorces and business break-ups. In a country that faces a growing economic crisis they may well be needed more and more. In the USA today only a third of new firms survive for four years and only 9% are still solvent after ten years. Most of those 9% are just hanging on by their financial fingertips.[12] A country that sees so many firms start up and fail needs a lot of lawyers to sort out all the mess of bankruptcy and redundancy.

Before becoming president, Donald Trump had been involved in 3,500 lawsuits.[13] Places with more stable and equitable economies need fewer lawyers because they have fewer Donald Trumps. The most equitable countries have the least: Japan has 17 times fewer lawyers than the USA, per person![14] Of course a minority of lawyers work in laudable sectors, seeking justice and defending the weak, but corporate lawyers are also essential for corporate corruption. When you ask who benefits most from inequality, one group who do are the corrupt.

Corruption is higher in countries with greater inequality because the rich have more to hide. As US economist Jeffery Sachs recently explained in relation to the wealthy in the USA, before listing a large number of crimes they have recently committed but gotten away with: 'Impunity means that the rich and powerful escape from punishment even when their malfeasance is in full view. Impunity is epidemic in America.'[15]

Sachs quotes examples of supporters of the very rich praising tax havens because they shelter 'their' wealth from the taxation of the 'predatory' US government. That wealth can then be 'invested' in countries like Brazil. Why do the rich care so much about money? Partly greed, but they also suffer enormous fear for their own families. Some of the wealth is invested to try to protect the children of the very rich, to help them to be rich in future (figure 4.2).

Inequality might not much help the 10%, or the 1%, or the 0.1%, but it might at the very least be thought to benefit the super-rich, the 0.01% and above. Details of the lives of the super-rich are generally kept secret, except when they divorce and then snippets come out in open court. One parent in a recent divorce case involving maintenance payments for a 7-year-old child requested that her ex-husband pay her £10,500 a year simply to fund her wine bill for the 210 bottles of wine at £50 each she needed each year to drink with the parents of her child's friends when the other children came to visit on 'play-dates'![16]

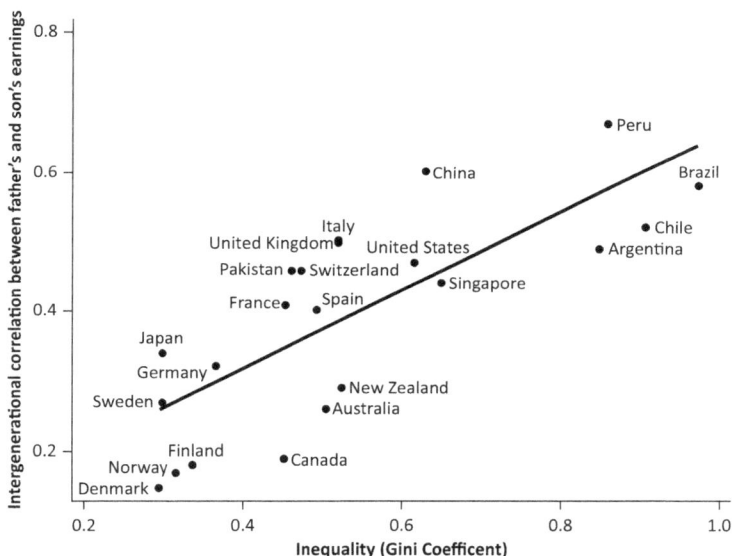

Figure 4.2 Intergenerational social mobility versus economic inequality, 2016

Source: Corak, M. (2016) *Inequality from Generation to Generation, the United States in Comparison*, IZA Discussion Paper 9929, May, http://ftp.iza.org/dp9929.pdf. Reproduced with permission from Miles Corak.

The court proceedings revealed that her 45-year-old ex-husband was maintaining homes in 'Cannes, Marrakesh, Miami and New York as well as London',[17] whereas the wife 'only' owned one home and so felt obliged to often use hotels. Another newspaper article talked of the husband's stellar spending habits and detailed his London homes including one costing £18m on which he intended spending £20m 'fabulously' refurbishing.[18] If he sees this as reasonable he won't be able to tolerate his son living on an average income or even many times an average income.

When the rich read stories about themselves many, such as the son-in-law of Donald Trump, conclude that 'the media [are] made up of socially insecure smartasses who glory in the human failings of the rich and powerful'.[19] But perhaps the wealthy feel so insecure and are such failures in many ways because they have so often led turbulent personal and business lives.

The newly wealthy are the few survivors, putting their survival down to skill, not luck; although they often say it was just bad luck when they fall. In the case of Donald's son-in-law, the real estate 'investor' Jared Kushner, he ensured his personal fortune by buying up to 11,000 properties for rent, involving 'a lot of evictions'.[20] Evictions require yet more lawyers. Who knows if Jared is happy with what he has done? But he will be known to the world for it.

In 2009 the Director General of the World Health Organization, Margaret Chan, identified the causes of the world's fuel, food and financial crises as the single-minded pursuit of economic growth, globalization and trade liberalization which were: 'creating massive problems of inequality, volatility and precarity. "Something," she said, "has gone horribly wrong".'[21]

The short-term benefits of increasing inequality always superficially appear greatest for those who are richest. In the USA the 400 richest families stood to gain most from the cuts to health care proposed by Donald Trump in 2017. In total these families will save $2.8bn a year if Obama's Affordable Care Act is repealed. That averages $7m per super-rich family per year. These are families that *each* receive an *annual* income of around $300m a year. It is perhaps worth pitying the very rich when you realize just how wedded to money they are and how hard they will fight to keep every last bit of it, including letting others suffer and die by denying them health care.

For the vast majority of American households, all those receiving less than $200,000 a year income (and mostly far less), there would be no tax savings from the repeal of the Affordable Care Act. Some 7 million US households would see their taxes rise as they would lose the insurance tax credits that were part of the bill. All this plays out along class and race lines: 'The 100 wealthiest Americans, none of whom are black, today own more wealth than the entire

African-American population combined.'[22] As I write in May 2017, the Act has not yet been repealed, but it will be preying on many Americans' minds.

Great inequality leads to great mental insecurity, for the rich as well as the poor, and especially for the young, who have more to feel insecure about. In the UK in 2017 an annual survey of wellbeing for young people aged 16 to 25 recorded its worst results since it had first been undertaken in 2009.[23] Asking about their hopes and dreams, it found that more than a third did not feel in control of their job prospects; that a third said they expected to have a worse standard of living than their parents; that more than a quarter no longer felt in control of their lives; a fifth said they did not have the ability to change their circumstances; a sixth said that they thought their life would amount to nothing, no matter how hard they try; and fully 42% said that traditional goals like owning a house or getting a steady job are unrealistic. It will be when they are a little older that they are most likely to suffer poor mental health (see figure 6.1). As Richard Wilkinson and Kate Pickett have explained at length, in high inequality countries where so many people see their life as worth so little, levels of violence are higher, and mental health is worse, including the mental health of the very affluent.[24]

Who Benefits from Inequality?

The rise in inequalities in the USA and UK began before Ronald Reagan and Margaret Thatcher were elected. But they were elected partly because of a change in sentiment that had occurred in the 1970s when a few people began to argue effectively for increasing inequalities. In the four decades before the 1970s the advocates of inequality had been largely shouted down. Sentiments change prior to a political change through the ballot box.

By 1978 in the USA, two years before Reagan was elected, Congress passed a tax bill that reduced capital gains tax enormously, to the benefit of the wealthy. It did this shortly after increasing pay-roll taxes regressively.[25] Since then inequality in the USA has risen to nearly match Brazil's, and inequality in the UK has risen to be the highest in Europe. It has become harder and harder each year to claim that anyone has greatly benefited from these trends, even those who at face value appear today to now be so well off. Children in the USA and the UK are now part of a generation that increasingly feels it is doomed, doomed because of the greed of the rich.

5

Where Do the Costs of Inequality Fall?

What's also clear is that climate change, together with mega-student debt and the loss of entry-level jobs to robots, will trigger a millennial revolt. Twenty-five-year-olds starting out in the workforce, and 35-year-olds with young children, are not going to settle for a septuagenarian president [Donald Trump] repeating climate falsehoods and squandering their future.

Jeff Sachs, 2016[1]

We now know that the *most affluent* people in the USA have a lower life expectancy if they live in states where inequalities are *higher*. 'Inequality was more negatively correlated with life expectancy for individuals in the highest income quartile, contrary to the prediction that inequality has the most adverse effects on the health of low-income individuals.'[2] Thus the health costs of inequality fall on the rich as well as the poor. The rich try very hard in the USA not to live near the poor, but the richer they are the more poverty they create around them.

Figure 5.1 shows, on its vertical scale, the 2014 infant mortality rates in the 50 states of the USA, Washington DC, and the 19 other affluent countries in the world for which these data were available in January 2017. Each of these 70 areas is drawn as a circle with area in proportion to its current population. The share of all income that was taken by the best-off 1% 31 years earlier (1983) determines the horizontal position of each circle. Those 31 years are roughly the length of a generation today. This is the first of a series of graphs demonstrating some of the long-term results of greater inequality. No one could have predicted most of these results and relationships in 1983, just as no one could have predicted all the effects of smoking and then beginning to cease smoking a generation earlier than that.

Figure 5.1 shows a very strong correlation in these affluent areas between infant mortality (which varied fourfold in 2014) and the take of the top 1% (which varied threefold in 1983) around the time when many of the mothers were themselves born. The 19 countries included in the graph are Australia, Canada, Denmark, Finland, France, Germany, Ireland, Italy, Japan, South Korea, the

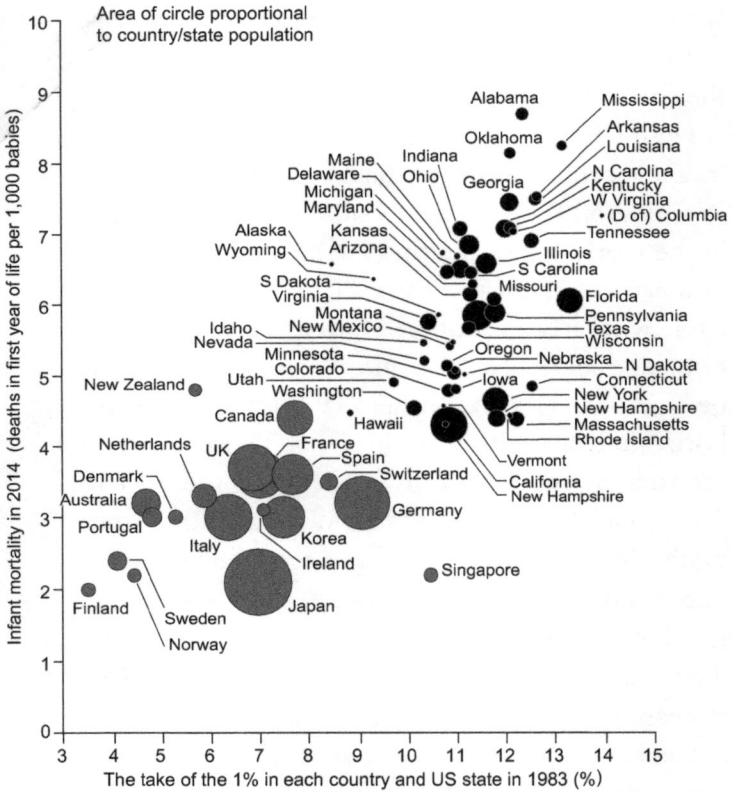

Figure 5.1 The take of the 1% and babies under one year dying a generation later, 19 countries and all US states

Source: World Wealth and Income Database, http://wid.world/, accessed December 2016. Infant mortality data from the Centers for Disease Control (USA) and Gapminder, https://www.cdc.gov/nchs/pressroom/sosmap/infant_mortality_rates/infant_mortality.htm.

Netherlands, New Zealand, Norway, Portugal, Singapore, Spain, Sweden, Switzerland and the UK, which are shown in addition to all the individual US states. All these countries now have higher overall life expectancy than the USA, not just lower infant mortality.

In 2016 it became apparent that life expectancy in the USA had begun to fall a year earlier in 2015, to 78.8 years (down from 78.9 years in 2014). Death rates had increased for eight of the ten leading causes of death in the USA.[3] These overall falls were blamed on declining access to health care for poorer Americans and wider societal factors, of which the most obvious is the growing economic inequality of recent decades and also inequality's current repercussions.[4] For middle-aged Americans mortality rates had failed to improve for almost twenty years due to 'a lack of hope'.[5]

Like the USA, the UK also saw a large rise in deaths in 2015.[6] One public health official explained to the BBC that social care cuts had an impact because: 'Cuts to meals on wheels services, for example, could mean more elderly people go through entire days without seeing anyone else, and if they are ill this would mean they deteriorate without anyone noticing.'[7] The rise in UK deaths seen in 2015 continued throughout 2016 and also involved a small rise in infant mortality. The large majority of the rise was due to more deaths among the vulnerable elderly who had seen no improvement in their health since 2011.

The 2012–16 increases in death rates in the UK has been partly linked to falls in welfare spending for poorer pensioners.[8] Pensioner poverty also ceased to improve after 2011 (see figure 7.2). But it has also been linked to low and stalling (or even falling) real health care expenditure in the UK.[9]

Between 2013 and 2014 as the inequality crisis in the UK deepened, the proportion of people over age 16 reported to have some feelings of depression or anxiety rose from 18.3% to 19.7%; for children it rose from 12.4% to 13.5%.[10] Small rises in the average measures of ill health can mask a bigger rise for people who are worse off and possibly a lower rise for those who are better off.[11]

The UK government saw its income from inheritance tax rise by a fifth in just one year in 2015 as so many elderly people died then; but because inheritance taxes are set so low in the UK and so few elderly people have much wealth, only £4.6bn was raised even with all the extra deaths.[12] However, by 2017 it became clear that the added deaths had removed £28bn from the pension fund liabilities of FTSE350 companies, and £310bn from future UK pension liabilities across the board.[13] As inequality grows and decisions are made to effectively reduce funding for health and care services, those who live longer suffer too, and they tend to be the very people who were better off when younger.

Figure 5.2 replaces infant mortality with a different variable, life expectancy at birth in 2015. Again we see the same trend both between countries and within the individual states of the USA. In any rich country today you are extremely unlikely to die in your first year of life, but you are still likelier to die earlier. In Mississippi life expectancy is currently only 75 years, and is in all likelihood now falling. In contrast, in Japan it is still steadily rising, and will be over 84 for men and women combined in 2017.[14]

Wherever economic inequality is higher, poverty is deeper and children suffer more. Child abuse and neglect become more common, especially in the states of the USA where inequality is higher.[15] One recent study of the 3,142 US counties concluded: 'Controlling for child poverty, demographic and economic control variables, and state-level variation in maltreatment rates, there was a significant linear effect of inequality on child maltreatment rates.'[16]

When life in unequal affluent countries becomes more precarious the children of the affluent also

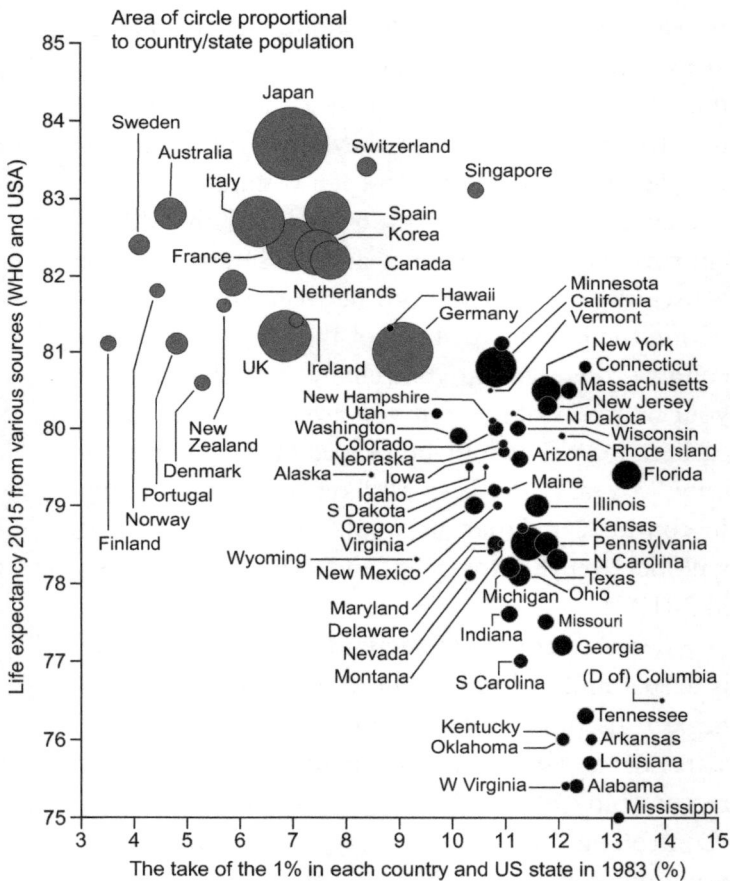

Figure 5.2 Take of the 1% and life expectancy in 19 countries and all US states

Source: World Wealth and Income Database, accessed December 2016. Life expectancy data from 'The Social Science Research Council Report: The Measure of America and World Health Organization Statistics (2016)'.

begin to worry more and suffer more. In 2016 it was reported that a fifth of Canadian university students had recently been diagnosed with anxiety or treated by a medical professional for anxiety within the previous year.[17] When polled at the same time, an eighth of UK university students believed they had a mental health condition. In contrast, only one in twenty older school students in Sweden suffer mental health problems.[18]

University students, especially in more unequal countries, are disproportionately drawn from better-off families. Despite this and because of the inequality in their country they are unlikely to feel that well off. The same is the case in slightly more equitable Canada. The two wealthiest Canadians now have *more wealth* than the combined wealth of the poorest 30% of Canadians, some 11 million people.[19] Similarly dramatic statistics can be produced for the UK and USA.

In the UK during 2016 the number of children living in poverty, mostly despite at least one parent having a job, rose by 200,000 to reach almost 4 million (28% of all children).[20] The UN Committee on Economic, Social and Cultural Rights explained that the UK government was choosing to lower taxes rather than secure children's rights. In 2017 calls to raise top tax rates to 65% in the UK began to spread,[21] following a recommendation by the British economist Sir Tony Atkinson.[22] However the UK government that was in power until 8 June 2017 had a manifesto commitment not to raise the top rate of income tax above its then current 45% level.

Access to health services for children worsened and the 2015–17 UK government repeatedly delayed publication of reports on adults dying shortly after reductions in their poverty relief payments.[23] The costs of gross inequality fall widely; the poor are the most obvious victims, but everyone is harmed in one way or another. The very rich have to pretend that inequality is not their problem while trying to hide from its consequences.

Poverty is concentrated in particular areas, but no area is free of it. In 2013 the then Prime Minister (David Cameron) visited a food bank in his own supposedly wealthy West Oxfordshire constituency. A decade earlier food banks were almost unheard of in the UK. He chose not to talk to any food bank users.[24] Many Conservatives believe that 'people live in poverty because they don't have the personal wherewithal to find a job, aspire to a better paid job, and mismanage their own money'.[25]

In the USA, unlike in the UK, the government routinely collects data on how many households cannot meet their basic food needs. In 2014 this was 48 million households or 14%.[26] In the USA food banks and food stamps have been in operation for longer, people die younger, including children; and recently the situation has been getting worse each year.

Between the years 2000 and 2016 the population living in US neighbourhoods defined as 'high poverty' doubled, from 7.2 million to 13.8 million. A 2017 study found that: 'Poor children are [now] more likely to live in high poverty neighbourhoods than poor adults, and much of the growth in concentration of poverty has not taken place in the largest US cities, the cities that attract most of our attention, but in the midsize metropolitan areas (population of half a million to a million people) that characterize where most Americans indeed live.'[27]

Smaller US cities have also been more affected by personal bankruptcy, which has increased dramatically in the USA since 1980.[28] Almost half (46%) of all people going bankrupt cited medical expenses as part of the reason; over a quarter (28%) as the primary reason.[29] The UK at least still has a National Health Service and so avoids bankruptcy due to unpaid medical bills, but both the UK and US now have rising student debt, which persists after bankruptcy.

Where Do the Costs of Inequality Fall?

Very recent research has found that people in more economically unequal states of the USA are more interested than most others in buying status symbols – positional goods which 'show how rich or successful they are compared to other people. . . . Someone who buys such goods may be particularly concerned to demonstrate their social status.' This includes Ralph Lauren clothing, designer boots and designer jewellery, which were found to have been searched for on the Internet more often in such states.[30] A degree from a more prestigious university is also a status good.

Research from a few years earlier had confirmed that overall consumption was higher in more unequal states.[31] This contributes to the bankruptcy rates, although medical problems and medical bills, divorce or loss of job are usually the final straw that leads to bankruptcy. For every additional low-income household in a US state, as compared to the number of high-income households, the annual bankruptcy rate of households rises by 0.5%.[32] We knew some of this a few decades ago, but most of what we now know about the extent of the harm done by inequality we have only come to realize in the last dozen years.

Loans to purchase consumer durables rose in the US as income inequality rose in the decades after

1980. A detailed study found that: 'Rising income inequality has been the largest contributor to the increase in consumer credit [in the United States].'[33] And at the same time total unsecured debt in the UK reached an all-time high in 2016, averaging almost £10,000 per household.[34]

Further studies have found that when US states are compared the 'results link violent crime to inequality in visible expenditure, but not to inequality in total expenditure',[35] as conspicuous consumption rises so do crime rates. Another study used US data to conclude 'that fads, fashions, and herd behavior should be more important at higher incomes'.[36] For instance, during the recent Californian drought in Montecito city,[37] rather than cut water consumption for their gardens, the super-rich simply paid the very steep fines imposed on them, or even paid for water to be tankered in to keep their gardens looking green and their swimming pools topped up.[38]

By now you should not be surprised to hear that the more economically *unequal* a county or state is, the greater is the average ecological footprint of its residents, and the more they pollute and waste. Figure 5.3 makes this very clear. It is for the same seventy areas as figures 5.1 and 5.2.

The environmental harm caused by economic inequality is staggering. Estimates published by Thomas

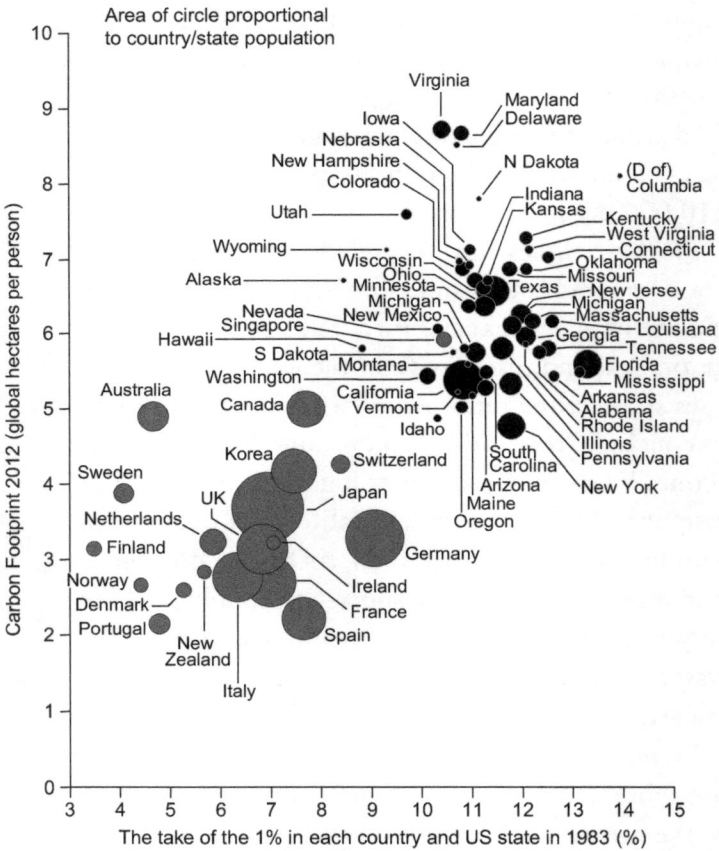

Figure 5.3 The take of the 1% in 1983 and average ecological footprint in 2012, 19 countries and all US states

Source: Global Footprint Network (2016) National Footprint Accounts 2016, ecological wealth of the 50 states of the USA, and the World Income and Wealth Database, http://footprintnetwork.org/documents/State_of_the_States_results_2015.xlsx.

Where Do the Costs of Inequality Fall?

Piketty and colleagues in 2015 suggested that someone in the second decile of the German income distribution contributes in pollution the equivalent of 7 tonnes CO_2 annually. In contrast, the carbon pollution of an individual in the top 1% in the USA is 318 tonnes CO_2 each, or 45 times as much.[39] The main reason for such a discrepancy is the use of private planes in the US, but the reason for the use of planes, and a lack of decent trains, is economic inequality promoting individualism and reducing social planning. In the end, though, we will all suffer from accelerated global warming and the rich with their waterfront properties and multiple investments in industries likely to be affected may well be especially susceptible themselves in the long run.

When inequality is high, the immediate costs of inequality fall disproportionately on the poor. The rich try very hard to avoid paying taxes. In the UK in 2009 the super-rich – people with assets worth more than £20m – paid £4.4bn in income tax, but that fell, with a little undulation, to £2.8bn, £3.0bn, £2.6bn, £3.9bn and £3.5bn in the following years. This is despite their overall incomes rising and the number of such very rich people increasing from 5,900 to 6,500 over that period.

The rest of the UK population saw tax bills increase by more than £23bn over this same 2009–14 period, to pay around £270bn in total now. The super-rich paid just 1.3% of all taxes in the UK by 2015.[40] That is hardly surprising as by 2016 there was not a single government (Conservative) MP representing any of the 99 most impoverished constituencies in the UK.[41] The political parties of the rich do not want to know about the poor.

The poorest fifth of households pay taxes in the UK that equate to 38% of their income while the richest fifth pay only 35% of theirs. This is due to the effect of indirect taxes such as VAT hitting the poorest hardest.[42] The UK is now *so unequal* that the wealth of the *five* richest families, standing at £28bn in 2016, is greater than that of all the families of the poorest *fifth*.[43]

The costs of inequality are great and widespread. An Oxford modern history professor foresees 'a poisoned public life, a democracy reduced to the tyranny of tiny majorities who find emotional satisfaction in a violent, resentful rhetoric while their narrowly-elected leaders strip away their rights and persecute their neighbours'.[44]

Inequalities are fractal. Most counties and cities contain as much inequality within them as within the country they lie in. In Scotland in 2015 the *four richest* families were worth a billion more than the *poorest fifth* of the population living there,[45] and male tycoons head almost all of the richest families.

The costs of inequality fall disproportionately on women and children, particularly when it comes to housing. A third of private rented properties in England were found not to be of a decent standard when inspected in 2014, whereas 86% of social rented homes are decent. And in England more and more children, especially children just living with their mothers, are being forced into these substandard homes.

Under a quarter of all families with dependent children lived in the private rented sector in England in 2004 (23%). But then, as private landlords bought up more and more properties, by 2015 that proportion had risen to over a third (36%). It is the poorest children who live in the worst privately rented homes. However, they are faring better than the 57,000 families with children living in bed and breakfast accommodation in England in 2016, who in turn were better off than the rising numbers of people who are living on the streets.[46] Politicians in more equitable countries in Europe simply do not allow such harm to happen so often. They don't tolerate it. They would be embarrassed by it.

Researchers carry on producing harrowing report after report on the effects of the poverty that is created by high rates of inequality. A review of almost all the studies to have looked at the effects of low income on mother's mental health found that as soon as the income of poorer mothers rose, the incidence of maternal depression fell and the mother was then able to be warmer and more encouraging to her children.[47]

Even young children understood and were made anxious by their parents living in poverty and this affected their relationships, as described by one 9-year-old boy in 2007:

> I was just trying to make her laugh and she was quite stressed because she like had no money at that moment and she said, she said stuff like 'Go up to your room now' and 'Would you stop it please' and 'I don't like the way you joke with me most of the time' and stuff. But I was only trying to make her feel better instead of being stressed.[48]

Having more money than others does not make you happier. You might end up buying 210 £50 bottles of wine a year just to get through the play-dates. All the key factors affecting health and happiness are relative. Recently economists from the LSE showed that: 'People adapt to higher levels of income over time, but, much more importantly, they also compare their own income to that of their peers.

Analysing data from the British Household Panel Survey, we find that life satisfaction is predicted mainly by an individual's income relative to that of others in their peer group as defined by age, gender and region. The same is true in Australia and Germany.'[49]

What is often not said is that in affluent countries with narrower income inequalities, public services tend to be better funded and that appears to improve people's mental health: people are better housed and better cared for by the state, getting around is less stressful, and they are treated better by their neighbours.

There are a huge number of different social costs that come with tolerating high inequality, many of which may initially sound surprising. One example is adoption, which is far more common in more economically unequal countries than more equal countries. In the year ending 31 March 2016 some 4,690 children were adopted in the UK whereas in the Netherlands with a population roughly four times lower, it is 28 children annually.[50] That is an *enormous* difference in the numbers of mothers having to give up their children.

So why do you not hear more about the costs of inequality? This could be because of the political cost. Newspapers and television stations in unequal countries are bought up by tycoons, their media then begin to spread their views. These frequently include the view that it is good to have wide inequalities. National broadcasters such as the BBC are afraid to report the consequences of inequality too much for fear that they will be privatized.[51]

Think tanks can often only do work they are funded to do. In unequal countries they increasingly become mouthpieces for the very rich. Universities are influenced, especially 'since "the monied interests" are able to exercise undue influence over university appointments in economics', where appointees agree with the views of the funder.[52] Political parties are bought by donation and promises of political and media support. However, because the costs of rising inequality are so high and escalate so much, the truth eventually tumbles out in fact after fact after fact. We are all losers when inequalities rise and all winners when they fall.

6

What Are the Alternatives to Inequality?

... progress is never permanent, will always be threatened, must be redoubled, restated, and reimagined if it is to survive ... people who believe in fundamental and irreversible changes in human nature are themselves ahistorical and naive.

Zadie Smith, 2016[1]

We have not suddenly had an evolutionary change in our human nature to make us now tolerate ever rising inequality. We know that pursuing greater profits at any cost is pathogenic and oppressive.[2] Workers become less productive, crime rises. We have *repeatedly* been forced to find alternatives to rising inequality in our many histories. As Zadie Smith reminds us, it is not us that change quickly, but the circumstances we find ourselves in.

Welfare states were developed to mitigate the harm caused by the greedy and to allow their businesses to continue to flourish. In the past it was more often physical illness that was exacerbated by higher economic inequality, and a sick workforce is less productive. Today it is mental illness. In the financial year 2013–14 over 1.7 million adults in England accessed NHS services for severe or enduring mental health problems. Almost a million were referred to psychological services for common but debilitating mental health problems such as depression and anxiety disorders.[3]

Compulsory psychiatric admissions rose by 70% between 1987 and 1995 and have remained high since.[4] Figure 6.1 shows that the mental health toll now falls most heavily on those aged 25–49 when considering the severest cases, although if you are still extremely seriously mentally ill after age 50 you are more likely to be sectioned to the highest security facilities. Seeking alternatives to inequality includes seeking alternatives to mass medication and incarceration, not just of the continuously rising but relatively small numbers detained under the Mental Health Act, 30% of whom are now secured in private mental hospitals.[5] People need financial security to have emotional security. They need to be treated fairly.

The alternatives to inequality involve greater sanity in place of the madness of accepting the

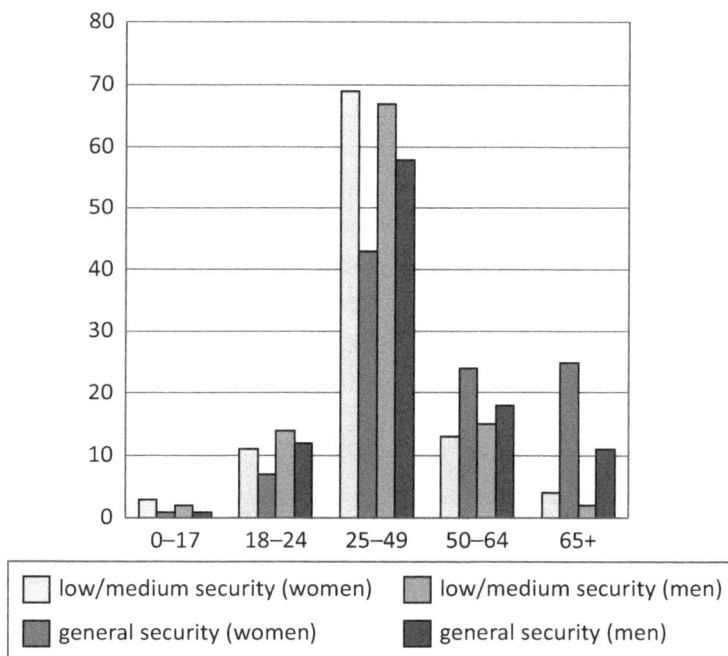

Figure 6.1 Age range of compulsorily detained patients by gender and security level (%), England and Wales, 2008

Source: Adapted from figure 9 in Mental Health Act Commission (2009) *Coercion and Consent*, London: TSO, p. 31.
Note: general security means patients with no specific security designation, this can imply higher than low/medium or not specified.

exploitation of the rich and trying to rationalize that exploitation as fair. The alternatives require understanding that it is in our human nature to expect to be treated fairly.

What Are the Alternatives to Inequality?

But what is fair? If custom demands that a particular job is highly paid, it is possible to end up with too few people doing that job because to employ more would be too expensive. The opposite of high inequality is not simply 'perfect equality'. The alternatives to high inequality require us to consider what fair remuneration is.

Here is a thought experiment. Think of a group of people you personally know. They could be your family, or your work colleagues, but they have to be in paid work. Within that group someone could end up working twice as many hours as in a normal working week, working up to 70 hours, so perhaps they should be paid twice as much. But no one can work more than that and function well. So hard work can justify being paid up to twice as much, but not more.

Let's carry the experiment on. Someone may be better at his or her job than another person; they may for instance be twice as good, implying that another is half as productive. But anyone who is less productive than that is not doing his or her job well so would be better off doing another job. Given that, it is not possible to easily argue for a greater reward than twofold for being especially able at your paid work.

Finally, some jobs are especially dirty, dangerous or degrading, or socially useful but not pleasant

to do and it may be hard to find someone will-
ing to do the work. If it is hard then it would make
sense to offer more money, but no job should be
so objectionable that more than double-pay is
required. This particular experiment leads to a particular conclusion about what might be fair.

The experiment shows it is possible to argue that
an 8:1 maximum inequality ratio can be defended.
Let's call this the 2×2×2 model. And that it would
be unfair for someone who is brilliant at their job,
works long hours and is doing something that is
very unpleasant, not to be paid that much more than
someone who is not so good at their job, works half
as many hours (a day) and is doing something that
many people would like to do.

You may wish to object to this and suggest
that there are a few people who are so exceptionally skilled that they deserve more, and that not
enough such people are available, so they need to be
encouraged by high pay. Or you might argue that
some others need to be compensated for getting so
little when they were training; but surely it would
have been better to give them more then? Or you
might argue that few people would set up a business if they could not earn much more than eight
times others, despite being exceptionally good at
something being a reward in itself.

What Are the Alternatives to Inequality?

Most people think that those with a job they consider to be especially skilled, say heart surgeons, should be highly paid for their skill. I would suggest that they should be paid more just because it is stressful. Most people recommend exceptionally high pay for people whom they do not know well, based on fantasies. People are not that different, there are no real superheroes.

Taking responsibility is essentially enjoyable. In contrast, jobs that are not enjoyable often involve low work control, monotony and shift work, all factors that increase your risk of having a stroke or heart attack, as well as depression.[6] It is ignorance of this that results in people being duped into thinking that top jobs require extraordinarily high levels of compensation. Would a heart surgeon really rather scrub the operating theatre clean, if not paid so much to be a surgeon?

We have allowed ourselves to be duped into believing some of us are worth much more than others, a discourse which has a superficial meritocratic ideology underpinning it. As a result there is little social solidarity in the most unequal of affluent countries, and an increasing number of people in younger and then middle age suffer from poor mental health. A meritocracy declares most people to be relatively worthless and hence inadequate.

What Are the Alternatives to Inequality?

The meritocratic myth is sustained despite it not being heart surgeons and human rights barristers that are the people receiving the highest remuneration in unequal countries – it's people doing actively socially harmful jobs like futures traders and advertising executives. And it is the lowly paid nurse who deals with the sobbing patient at night and the junior solicitor who goes to the immigration detention centre who both have the harder jobs, not the lauded surgeon or the barrister above them in the respective pecking order.

Most highly paid jobs are relatively cushy. In contrast, exhausting and soul-destroying jobs tend to be very poorly paid. Most highly successful people have just been lucky.[7] Many more, equally competent and hard working, have just not been. How much more should you receive for luck? Fortunately, there is no need to work through all these hypothetical ideas. We can simply look at what actually happens around the world to see what the alternatives are, what is possible.

The UK and USA *could* enjoy the current low rates of inequality in Scandinavian countries or in Japan, or the still relatively low rates in the Netherlands or Switzerland, or even Germany and France. They could even be a little bit more imaginative than that in future. If trends in economic inequality were to follow the trends within progressive countries in racial equality, sexual equality and so on, what might be possible that we currently don't enjoy?

What *were* the drawbacks of allowing women to go to universities, of seeing people with darker skin as not inferior? So what might *be* the drawbacks of ensuring that no one is poor and no one is unnecessarily rich in future? Much greater progress may occur in the coming decades than we currently even dare to dream is possible. What most prevents progress is the view that it is impossible, not the wealth and power of the rich.

In Finland, the Netherlands, Kenya and Canada experiments are underway to begin to understand the impact of handing out a basic income to people. It gives psychological as well as financial help (according to evidence already gathered in an experiment in Uganda).[8] Some on the left are concerned that giving people an income for doing nothing allows those on the right who support a basic income to perpetuate many other inequalities; but most right-wingers oppose basic income.

The very first Canadian basic income experiments in the 1970s found that two groups did choose to do a little less paid work: 'New mothers were using their additional income to extend their maternity leave and spend more time with their infants, and teenage boys were using that income to stay in school.'[9] Today this would not be seen as a criticism. And that shows we are changing how we think.

At the global level, progress on reducing inequalities is slow, but it is now underway, including in China. As mentioned earlier in the book, inequality dominated the January 2017 World Economic Forum in Davos. Business leaders are becoming scared of popular revolt.[10] The Chinese premier went to Davos for the first time, perhaps because of similar concerns. At that meeting he and they heard that giving everyone a basic income was the same as insisting that everyone wear a seatbelt while driving, rather than trying to target the wearing of seatbelts (or 'benefits') to those you think most likely to crash. The global costs of not having basic incomes were declared at Davos to exceed $1tn a year.[11]

In January 2017 the very rich men at Davos were unusually open to suggestions over what needed to be done. However, they would not countenance helping trade unions bargain for better wages and preferred unlikely solutions: 'calculated to spare corporations and the wealthiest people from having to make any sacrifices at all, as if there is a way to be found to tilt the balance of inequality while those at the top hang on to everything they have'.[12] Christine Lagarde, the managing director of the International Monetary Fund, countered: 'It's an opportune time to put in place the policies we know help. When you have a real crisis, what kind of measures do we take to reduce inequality? It probably means more redistribution.'[13] Sceptics wondered whether this meant just enough redistribution to prevent mass protest.

On the reduction that has been seen in extreme poverty, Oxfam have explained that if economic growth between 1990 and 2010 had been 'pro-poor' then there would be around 386 million people living in extreme poverty today rather than over 1.1 billion.[14] That was the alternative to growing inequality that was *not* chosen in the 1980s. As Oxfam now repeatedly say, anyone who cares about ending poverty has to get serious about inequality.

In 2016, in New York, fifty millionaires wrote a letter to the state's Governor, Andrew Cuomo, asking him to increase their taxes because they thought inequalities had grown too high. They wanted to be taxed more to give local government more funds to renew basic infrastructure and to increase the incomes of the poorest. The group included Abigail Disney, granddaughter to Walt Disney, and Steven Rockefeller, a fourth-generation member of that very wealthy family.[15] Taxes are just one way of reducing inequalities, but the rich *asking* for tax increases is new.

For taxes to work they have to be founded on shared and collectively recognized values. To work they require a shared sense of reciprocal trust, an atmosphere of compromise and mutual recognition.[16] When that atmosphere has been poisoned, tax avoidance becomes the norm.

Those who cannot avoid paying tax are envious of others who don't pay tax, envious of both the non-contributing poor – who are a group particularly not to envy – and envious of the tax-avoiding rich. While those who have too much often do feel guilty about their tax-avoiding behaviour. Recent studies have found that in lab tests on the effects of inequality 'guilt parameters were greater than envy parameters in the majority of our subjects' and 'regardless of whether subjects themselves won or lost, average subjective well-being was attenuated for unequal compared with equal outcomes'.[17]

Unless they are psychologically damaged, people who win more in unequal societies recognize the unfairness and become less happy because of how they affect others. Associating only with people of similar wealth is a mechanism for reducing that stress. The results of increasing numbers of studies such as these have been widely reported in the press as: 'Your happiness isn't only dependent on your own situation – it's also influenced by what's happening to the people around you.'[18]

One alternative to inequality is more happiness. However, if reducing inequality was simple, and it was clear to us all that it was in all our interests, it would have already happened. In more inequitable countries many believe that someone very obviously much poorer than you can't be really like you, must be less deserving, possibly an *inferior human*. At the other extreme, we often gloat when disaster hits the wealthy – because when the gaps between us are wide, sympathy is in short supply.

A very recent US psychological study questioned 2,591 people in public places frequented by the affluent, in some cases next to a homeless person, in other cases not. It found 'that individuals are significantly less likely to support redistributive policies in the presence of a poor person in an affluent setting. ... Ultimately, changing minds may require cognizance of context.'[19] Some people in very unequal places have come to accept the inequality around them as justified, or unfair just to people like them.

Most people tend to consider what they see around them as normal, not strange. So if you live in a more equitable society it is not hard to understand the arguments for promoting equality. In a more unequal setting, if you are better off, it is hard not to try to justify your own affluence, especially when directly confronted with some of its repercussions. It is understandable to go on the defensive and to claim that your situation is merited, using the meritocracy myth. How else can you step past homeless people as you walk home and not worry?

To perpetuate inequality people have to be fooled into believing they are hard done by, when in fact they are better off. Here is a recent example. In December 2016 a survey of American voters found that a majority of men who had voted for Donald Trump thought that American women were better off than American men. They did not come to these views by themselves or by observation – they were fed these lines.

If you can persuade a better-off group, such as white American men, to believe that they are relatively worse off, then you damage support for reducing *actual* inequalities. The report of that particular survey included a quote from a retired white American police officer claiming: 'It's easier being a woman today than it is a man. The white man is a low person on the totem pole. Everybody else is above the white man.'[20]

What Are the Alternatives to Inequality?

You might think, 'how can a white US ex-policeman not see what should be clear to him?' *But you are not him*. For similar reasons you may find it hard to see how fascism can rise, *but you were not there*. Among rich nations that have been compared, support for a 'strong leader who does not have to bother with elections' grew the most in the USA between 1995 and 2014 with a third of those surveyed expressing such support by 2015. In contrast, the proportion fell in Sweden over that same time period, having been lower to begin with. Only a third of young adult Americans now believe that it is 'essential to live in a country that is governed democratically', as compared to 60% of young Swedes.[21]

One alternative to high inequality is fascism. When people are very *unhappy*, they can be more easily persuaded to vote for far-right parties. They can be convinced that putting a bullying, aggressive tyrant into power will aid them, believing that such men (and the occasional women) really do have others' interests at heart. Thankfully elections reveal that support for the far-right is still low in most European countries, even though we know that such parties can gain a few votes in the most equitable of countries, with the Danish People's Party wining 21% of the popular vote in 2015; the

Finns Party gaining 18% in Finland in 2015; and the (so-called) Democrats gaining 13% in the most recent (2014) Swedish general election.[22]

The *New York Times* study that was used to draw up figure 6.2 did not include Norway, but its 'Progress Party' gained 16% of the popular vote there in 2013, more than the 13% the UK Independence Party (UKIP) gained in the 2015 British general election. Figure 6.2 shows all these results, plotted against inequality, as measured thirty years earlier, again taking a long-term view. Back then there was very little support for far-right parties, but gradually opinions have shifted, and shifted most where inequality was highest a generation before, where the brakes were taken off early.

Figure 6.2 can be compared to the graphs showing rates of infant mortality and life expectancy in the last chapter (figures 5.1 and 5.2). Here votes for Donald Trump in the 2016 US presidential election are included as far-right because, by any international assessment, Donald Trump's rhetoric in the 2016 election campaign was at least as far to the right as any nationalistic European politician.

All alternatives to high inequality rely on activism and the fascist alternative is no different. Recent research has shown that support for the US Tea Party that pre-dated Trump's rise to power

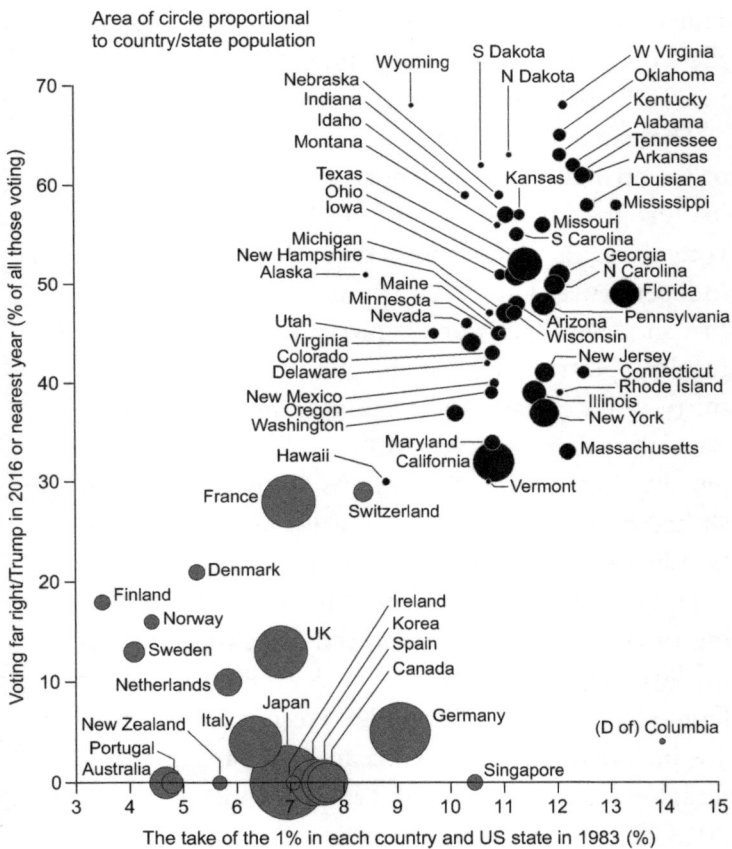

Figure 6.2 The take of the 1% in 1983 and voting far right in 2016, 19 countries and all US states

Source: World Wealth and Income Database, http://wid.world/, accessed December 2016; and http://www.nytimes.com/interactive/2016/05/22/world/europe/europe-right-wing-austria-hungary.html & http://www.nytimes.com/elections/results/president.

depended on activism. For each Tea Party protestor who attended an anti-tax rally the number of additional people later voting Republican in the local areas rose by between 7 and 14 votes.[23] The researchers who discovered this invented an ingenious new method of testing the effects of protest by whether rain intervened to dampen the size of protests. They helped prove that protesting is effective. However, while activism and protesting matter, it is the underlying economic context that is most important in determining the likelihood of fascism rising, as figure 6.2 demonstrates.

What the figure shows is that, in general, the more economically unequal a state or country was in 1983, the higher was far-right voting in the years immediately up to and including 2016. The main exceptions to this regularity are France, where the National Front does better than would otherwise be expected, Germany where the AfD (*Alternative für Deutschland*) polled only 5% in 2013, Singapore which has no far-right minority party, but is governed by a very right-wing majority party[24] and Washington DC where Trump polled only 4% of the vote in 2016. Washington is a largely poor city in which half the population are African American.

West Virginia and Wyoming were the most far-right voting states in the USA, and far more

101

right-wing than any of the countries compared here, with the latter also being a slight anomaly to the general trend as Wyoming is not one of the most economically unequal of US states. In Wyoming one white lady who said she voted for Trump also said: 'I'm hoping [Trump] will be impeached and his vice president will run the country . . . [Pence] is less evil than the other ones.'[25] Mike Pence was standing for vice president alongside Trump.

When people are forced to vote for whom they think might be 'less evil', many choose not to vote. Only 57% of people in Wyoming chose to vote. The lowest proportion was 38% in Hawaii.

The highest proportion choosing to vote at the most recent presidential or general election was 93% of people in Singapore. It is an outlier because voting is, in essence, compulsory in Singapore. If you don't vote you have to pay a fine to be allowed to ever vote again. Voting is high in Australia for similar reasons, but also in Denmark and Italy because they fit the general trend of a higher turnout to vote in economically more equitable countries and which also tend to have a wider, more interesting, and less 'evil', set of politicians to vote for. See figure 6.3 for how the inequality context appears to influence turnout in democratic elections.

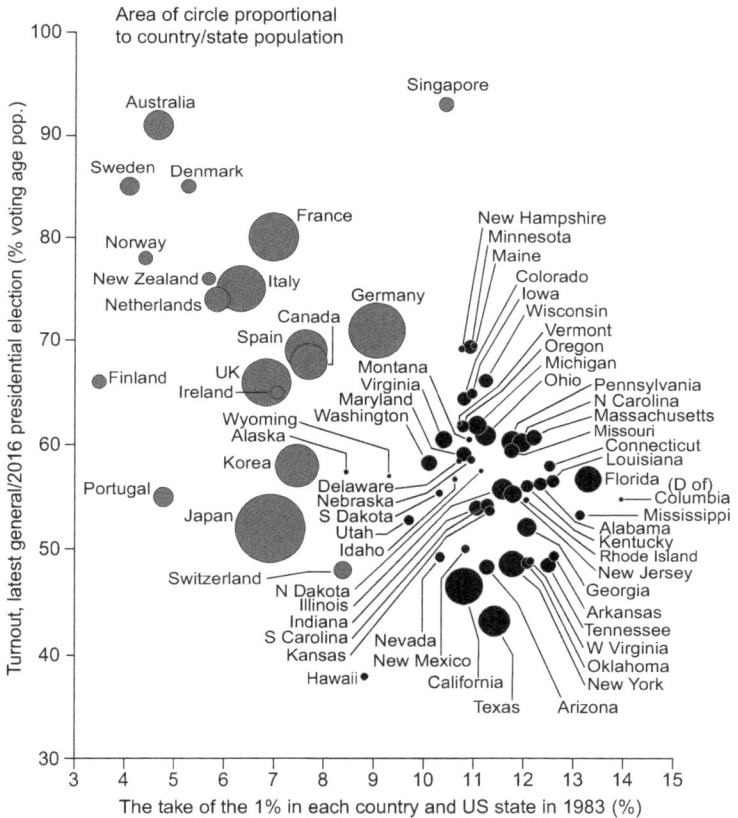

Figure 6.3 The take of the 1% in 1983 and electoral turnout in 2016, 19 countries and all US states

Source: World Wealth and Income Database, http://wid.world/, accessed December 2016; and http://www.electproject.org/2016g

What Are the Alternatives to Inequality?

Great economic inequality results in bad decisions being made. It reduces people's motivations to vote, and when they do vote they are given less choice and are more poorly informed. Campaigning is less honest. The voters in unequal countries tend to be offered politicians that suggest just slower or faster increasing – but always increasing – inequality. Then, having grown accustomed to living with the social, economic and environmental consequences of great economic inequality, most voters come to believe it is inevitable.

In more unequal countries voters are less likely to realize how inequality contributes to problems such as breathing in pollution and sitting in traffic because you commute a long way to work, because living near work is too expensive or too cheap and too dangerous. Politicians in more unequal countries are more likely to dismiss alternatives to traffic pollution as undesirable.

In all of Europe traffic congestion is worst in the UK.[26] This finding appeared in a report commissioned for the UK's Department of Transport that also determined that car congestion in the UK worsened between 2010 and 2015. It was released after the Chancellor of the Exchequer, Philip Hammond, criticized funding for cycling in London. Previously, as Transport Secretary, Hammond had claimed that cycling was trivial and should not be a part of his department's remit.[27]

The greatest pollution in the UK is caused by people living just outside the M25 motorway around London. The same is found in the suburban and rural areas around New York City in the USA.[28] If you live in the UK or USA this may sound trivial to you. You might say, 'What are people complaining about?' But that is because you have become used to the congestion, pollution and inequality. Air pollution kills *ten times* as many people as die in road crashes, more in London than anywhere else in Europe.[29]

In contrast, local government in Barcelona is considering plans to make large areas of the city only accessible to pedestrians and cyclists. Within those areas, if cars or lorries need access, they must travel no faster than 7 miles an hour. Some 300 km of new cycle lanes are planned for the city, increasing the provision of cycle lanes fourfold, and more bus provision is also planned so that no one is ever more than 300 metres from a bus stop in that area.[30] Spain is more equitable than the UK, especially the Catalonia region, around and including Barcelona.

The alternatives to great inequality come in many forms. The public transport alternatives to cars are *less* well explored in countries with greater economic inequalities, partly due to lobbying from the astonishingly rich. Between 2010 and 2015 the number of billionaires in the world with investments in fossil fuels rose from 54 to 88 and the fortunes of this subset of billionaires rose from $200bn to $300bn over the same time period[31] – a period when other billionaires did not fare so well, as the next chapter explains.

However, there is hope in even the most unequal of affluent countries. The young are ready for progressive alternatives. In the USA three quarters of adults aged under thirty want alternative wind and solar energy sources prioritized over coal and oil.[32] It was mostly the old that voted for the regressive alternatives that Brexit and Trump offered in 2016.

Once progressive alternatives to inequality are taken up they are quickly accepted as normal and there always comes a time when we forget that all inequalities were once passionately argued for by their advocates, from the time of the very first slave holder justifying his slave holding through to the rich today trying to justify their riches.

7

When Will the Fall in Inequality Become Clear?

... crisis may not be as exceptional as economists assume, which explains why they are often hard pressed to explain their failed predictions.

Susana Narotzky and Niko Besnier, 2014[1]

It is only clear that inequalities have fallen long after the fall has begun. Often the fall begins due to an economic crisis, and crises are becoming more frequent. At the point of crisis there can be a hiatus. In China the take of the 1% peaked in 2008 at 13.5%, by 2015 it had fallen to 12.7%.[2] Soon China could be the largest economy in the world, and one still becoming more equal. The USA is more unequal than China by any measure, and is clearly already in crisis.[3]

Frequently we think that a crisis must result in the beginnings of a change, but then the old order appears to reassert itself. However, we are now in an era where we have begun to expect more crises to emerge, as part of a general pattern of crises that will continue for as long as we do not address growing or high inequalities. Economists now avoid making predictions of future stability.

We too easily forget how wrong all leaders of greatly unequal countries are when they proclaim stability. Gordon Brown, UK Chancellor of the Exchequer from 1997 to 2007, opened the new European offices of Lehman Brothers in 2004, saying, 'I would like to pay tribute to the contribution you and your company make to the prosperity of Britain.' He continued to be extremely positive about UK/USA financial services, including when he addressed bankers in his annual Mansion House speech in 2007:

> I congratulate you on these remarkable achievements, an era that history will record as the beginning of a new golden age for the City of London. I believe it will be said of this age, the first decades of the 21st century, that out of the greatest restructuring of the global economy, perhaps even greater than the industrial revolution, a new world order was created.[4]

Three months later came the first run on a British bank for 150 years. The bank was ironically called Northern Rock. The following year Lehman Brothers filed for bankruptcy and the UK government had to bail out the Royal Bank of Scotland, Lloyds TSB and Halifax Bank of Scotland (HBOS). Ironically a new world order *was* created as the rich world became a little poorer, starting with the poorest in the rich countries.

Nine years after Brown's speech, reports that the global wealth of the very richest was falling began to circulate. In March 2016, the Forbes 30th annual billionaires guide found that the number of billionaires in the world had dropped from 1,826 to 1,810. The total wealth of those that were left had fallen by $570bn to roughly $6.5tn. They had been rocked by 'market turbulence' including falling oil prices. This was the first fall in their wealth since 2009.[5] It might be untrue, an artefact of some statistical error. Or it might be true but not last long. Or it might be part of the turn. In March 2017 the number of billionaires was reported by Forbes to have risen again, along with their average wealth, but its stock market foundations were looking more and more shaky. It is foolish to predict, but equally foolish not to speculate.

The number of billionaires living in Africa fell from 28 in 2014 to 21 in 2016,[6] while the numbers in China continued to rise even as the 1% there took less overall. The American billionaires were 'suffering' most of all. One, Donald Trump, was reported to have lost a quarter of his wealth during 2016 due to the falling value of his holdings at the top end of the New York property market.[7] The March 2017 figures revealed great turbulence, with almost as many losing great sums of money as those making more and more.

Below the billionaires, are the multi-millionaires, a group who also appeared to have lost out recently according to various 'rich-lists'. In May 2017 the *Sunday Times* newspaper revealed a 14% rise in the wealth of the 1,000 richest people living in Britain. That rise was less than the fall in the value of the pound over that same year, the currency in which their wealth was measured. In real terms the richest in the UK were becoming less rich. This does not mean that the fall in inequality has now begun, but if it had – it would be easy to miss. The *Sunday Times* did not point it out. We tend to dismiss any signs of falling inequalities. We tend to look out for bad news, not good. We concentrate on the richest of billionaires becoming richer and not on the rest or the millionaires. And we can often miss slower trends that suggest a new era is coming.

In October 2016 the largest drop in sales of rich men's jewellery – luxury Swiss watches – was reported, a 16% fall in exports compared to October 2015. This was part of a long-term trend, established shortly after the 2009 financial crash – of decelerating rises followed by actual declines in luxury watch sales. The most basic luxury watch costs $5,000.[8] Figure 7.1 suggests it could be an early sign of the fall in inequality beginning. There is growing evidence from the United States that conspicuous consumption among the 1% fell rapidly after 2008.[9] The rich now have less money to waste

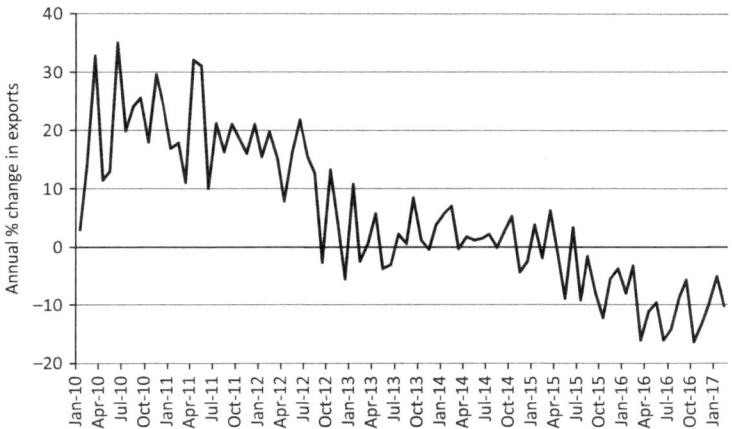

Figure 7.1 Year-on-year percentage change in global Swiss watch exports, 2010–2017

Source: Federation of the Swiss Watch Industry via Bloomberg, https://www.bloomberg.com/view/articles/2016-12-12/middle-class-angst-is-depressing-swiss-watch-sales updated through to 2017 using data from http://www.fhs.swiss/eng/statistics.html

111

on fancy watches and similar ostentation. As turbulence increases and crisis becomes more common the rich are less sure of their future.

We will probably see the fall in inequality begin at the top of the income and wealth scale, not at the bottom, and after life for the poorest has first worsened. This is what happened before in the 1920s and 1930s and it may be what is just starting to happen now. It happens partly because rising wealth inequalities can never continue indefinitely. In the year to October 2016 sales of individual properties within London 'worth' more than £10m fell by 86%; and outside of London, from ten properties in 2015 to none being sold for such huge prices in 2016.[10] In May 2017 it became clear that values across London for all properties had fallen. The fall in UK wealth inequality could have already begun.

A fall in inequality can begin without policy and political changes, but they help sustain it. In December 2016 the City of Portland, Oregon, announced that it would surcharge companies that paid their CEOs more than 100 times their median workers' pay.[11] In 2016 in the USA the average pay of the top 500 CEOs had fallen to 335 times the income of the average worker. That is incredibly high but in 2014 it was 373 times, although this compares to 42 times in 1980 and 107 times in

1990.[12] When these facts were announced, a senior fellow of the right-wing Adam Smith Institute, wrote:

> What 500 people among 340 million get paid makes so little difference to income inequality as to be effectively indistinguishable from zero. . . . Has income inequality increased? Most assuredly. Is this a bad thing? Up to you to decide that.[13]

He turned out to be a hesitant lone voice, and that too could be a sign that the tide has turned. Almost all other commentators now believe inequalities have grown too high. In the UK the average CEO of big British companies was paid 131 times average workers in 2016 (up from 47 times in 1998). The Prime Minster said she would consider introducing new rules to ensure such pay ratios were published for all companies.[14] She is no radical, but she recognizes that moral sentiment has changed and she has to at least *pretend* that she cares.

The turning of the tide is not an easy thing to see, especially when the sea is rough. What happens at first is that the tide comes in more and more slowly, just a slowing down in increasing inequality. It is not obvious when the waters begin to recede because of the variable uprush and backwash of each wave and because (in the absence of an economic tsunami) the tide ebbs back at first slowly.

We dismiss any apparent small falls in inequality as being only temporary, just blips. And we often don't notice when the calls and then clamour for change become a cacophony. We think, 'people have been saying these things for years, and it never makes any difference'. We don't even notice when it becomes common to read of bankers themselves saying that the banks need to be fundamentally changed; but they have started to say this, following a change in mainstream opinion, a change in the general moral sentiment.

We need publicly run and accountable local banks, so we are not so reliant on the huge, irresponsible corporate banks based in London and New York. Many progressive manifestos now call for the largest banks in the USA and UK to be split up.[15] Previously staid commentators now ask, 'can we reverse the financialisation of our economy?' And respond, 'realism will require radicalism'.[16]

It is now commonly understood that in very unequal countries most economic growth comes not from new production but from trade in existing assets, in property, in land, in *objets d'art*, in derivatives and 'futures' and through rent. 'Money is "made" simply out of the ability to own.'[17]

This becomes precarious and so the 2016 UK Conservative administration stopped buy-to-let tax relief for smaller landlords. Then UK banks dramatically cut their lending to those landlords in spring 2017 following the introduction of new affordability tests.[18]

The alternatives to rising economic inequality are already being tried out in more equitable countries. Even in a very unequal country like the UK there have been calls for 'a moratorium on crash-related home evictions and [to] rebuild the ... stock of social housing'. This was just one of twenty similar proposals made by the New Economics Foundation in 2008, the year of the Great Financial Crash.[19] Few have been taken up in the UK, but hardly any of them were even being discussed a decade earlier.

Within unequal countries you can now look to the new politics of Scotland where the independence campaign has spawned dozens of new organizations, one of which, *Common Weal*, produced hundreds of proposals including twenty-four just to reduce inequalities.[20] Or you can also look to Bernie Sanders's campaign in the USA which he lost, but not (it turned out) because Hillary Clinton was more electable.

There is a change in the air. It is the highest paid occupations of all that now receive the most disdain. The highest paid people after CEOs and a few other company board level posts are bankers. Across Europe the number of bankers paid more than a million euros a year rose from 3,178 in 2013 to 3,865 in 2014[21] and then 4,133 in 2015.[22] That rising inequality led to instability and then the vote for Brexit in 2016.

The preliminary figures for 2015 revealed that 971 people working in just four of the large US banks in London received more than a million euros each in 2015, eleven of those who were working for Goldman Sachs received more than €5m.[23] Before 2016 more than *three quarters* of all the top paid bankers in Europe worked in London, 2,926 in 2014; more then ten times the next highest number, 242, in Germany.[24] But by March 2017 the press began to report that the number of bankers receiving this much in 2016 had fallen by a third, and that most of those who had lost out worked in London.[25]

In London in 2014, sixteen bankers were paid more than €10m that year, with one paid almost €25m.[26] By 2015 that top salary, including perks, had risen to €34m, of which 99% was made up of bonuses! Most UK voters had had enough of what was happening to them as the rich got richer, as schools and hospitals were underfunded and as housing for the 99% became harder to get. But the voting public were told it was EU regulations and poorer immigrants that we needed to rid ourselves of, not such gross inequality. One way in which we know inequalities are approaching a peak is when they result in tumultuous political outcomes. It was not poor immigrants that were prising people out but rich landlords trying to increase their wealth further. And it was the rich who funded the political parties that ensured public services were so badly funded in the UK as compared to all other countries in Western Europe.

Before the June 2016 Brexit vote a third of London's highest paid bankers worked for US banks. As a result of the vote, by early 2017 it became clear that Goldman Sachs would halve the number of investment bankers it employed in London from 6,000 to 3,000, moving 1,000 to Frankfurt and others to New York, France, Spain and Poland.[27] They will not be paid so much in mainland Europe. In Paris there are now plans to build 200 km of new public railway and sixty-eight stations to cope with the influx of jobs coming from London.[28]

Soon we will read detailed reports of how the number of top paid bankers in London has fallen. Then we will ask why might a banker in London have demanded to be paid almost £25m for a year's work in 2014 and so much more than that in 2015? Even assuming a 50-hour week and just a few holidays a year, this pay is £10,000 an hour. In 2016, one accomplished banker who has worked for many of the world's largest banks described how in one of his jobs he 'reported to four individuals and none of them had any idea of what I was doing, nor what I was supposed to be doing'.[29] Highly critical of many aspects of current banking, including the low level of banker expertise and integrity, he wrote a book explaining how we need healthy banks, not ever more profitable ones.

Bankers may believe that they are worth more than a thousand times the people who clean the buildings they work in, if they see them as expendable. Those bankers probably see themselves as uniquely valuable and *not* overpaid. Perhaps the highest paid bankers think they are as valuable as Martin Sorrell – the CEO of WPP plc, a London based advertising and PR company – who received £65m in 2016 for a year's work.[30] Or they may realize that the tide has turned on such perverse logic. Martin Sorrell's pay is now set by the shareholders of WPP to fall rapidly. We will know the tide is turning through a thousand actions like this.

When Will the Fall in Inequality Become Clear?

For almost everyone who is very well paid there is someone who is paid much more than them and who does not work harder or have another reasonable justification for being worth so much more. Above the highest paid are those tiny few whose wealth produces an income from 'investing' that is far greater than the highest salaries in the world. This can be used as further self-justification for those who are not billionaires as to why they should be paid more.

All the logic used to try to justify inequality is perverse. When people become extremely rich they tend to turn to philanthropy to ease their worries and boost their self-esteem. In 2010 Warren Buffett and Bill Gates, created the 'Giving Pledge', inviting the wealthiest people in the world to pledge more than half of their wealth to charitable causes either during their lives or in their wills. In January 2017 there were over 150 pledges.

At first philanthropy appears worthy, but later, as inequalities rise it begins to look selfish. The *average* net wealth of each of these 150 people is almost $6bn. And their 'pledges' are often simply tax avoidance.[31] Others begin to ask: Why do they think they are best placed to decide how to spend that money for the common good? So the rich try to present themselves in a better light. A rise in humility among some at the top is sorely needed.

Since 2012 in the UK it has been the poorest fifth of households that have seen the smallest percentage rise in their incomes, around 3% by 2015.[32] Over time more and more poorer households include adults in work, often doing mundane jobs such as acting as a security guard.[33] Families in the UK and USA are now often unable to give their children a decent standard of living. For every *two* children that were poor in the UK in 2015, *three* are predicted to be poor by 2021.[34]

The projected increase in inequality affecting children more than any other group is shown in figure 7.2. This is the proportion of children living in households with below 60% of median household income. Increasing numbers of those children will live in poorer areas of the UK, places like Blackburn in Lancashire, but also the centre of London.[35] Even as inequality reduces as incomes at the top begin to fall, absolute poverty can rise. The same occurred before; as shown by Seebohm Rowntree's comprehensive reports on poverty in York published in 1901 and 1941, between which years inequalities fell, but absolute poverty at first rose.

High and rising poverty changes the mood of a nation. Almost a quarter of people (23%) in the UK were living in poverty in 2014, including a higher proportion of children. After housing costs

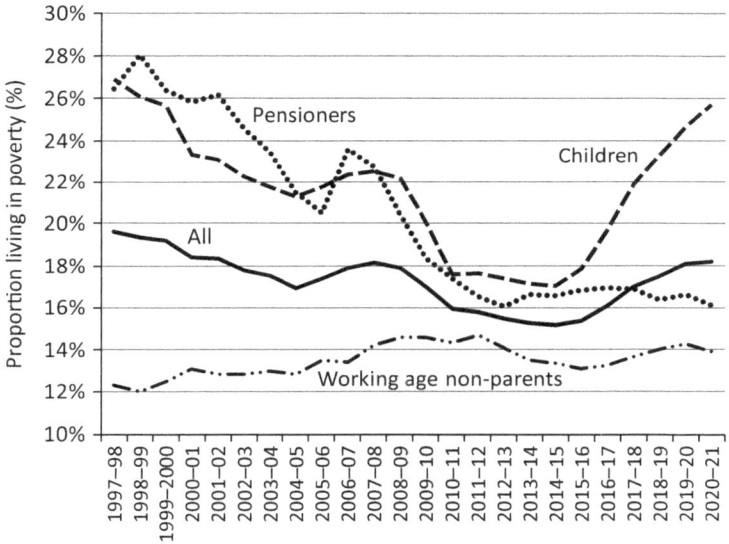

Figure 7.2 Relative poverty rates by household type, UK, 1997–2021

Source: Browne, J. and Hood, A. (2016) *Living Standards, Poverty and Inequality in the UK: 2015–16 to 2020–21*, Report 114, London: Institute for Fiscal Studies, figure 3.9, http://www.ifs.org.uk/publications/8171. Reproduced with permission of Andrew Hood. *Note*: Incomes measured before housing costs have been deducted. Relative poverty is below 60% of median household income in the current year. Pensioners are those aged 65 or over. Projection uses the IFS tax and benefit microsimulation model.

are taken into account that proportion rose to 28% and is projected to reach 36% of all UK children by 2021.[36] Around 1.75 million people were convicted of crimes back in 2014, mostly associated with poverty, and mostly committed by young adults, often with the victims being other young adults. The UK prison population rose to 94,868 that year – per person that was the highest rate in all of Europe and the highest ever in the UK.

People become disgusted when shareholders profit from rising poverty. Between May 2010 and April 2015 the prison and security firms G4S and Serco were paid £2.1bn by the UK government for carrying out work that had been privatized. Meanwhile, the police force saw its numbers cut from 168,031 officers to 149,139 over that same time period, which has even resulted in attempts to set up small private police forces.[37]

As inequality rises so too does serious crime. The British police now deal with over 1 million cases of domestic abuse each year and roughly half a million mental health related incidents each year. All this coincides with rising inequality, which is why the *UK Justice Policy Reviews*, from which these figures are drawn, also include statistics on inequality.[38] And it is all not as bad as in the United States of America.[39]

The fall in inequality will be apparent not so much in your pay packet, but when things around you begin to feel different; when people notice that they are living in a place governed with more empathy, greater respect, justice, kindness, fun and love than they currently see or experience. A more equal society is one in which everyone's needs are better met without harming the environment or damaging the prospects for future generations. And those above you have less and are less mean.

When equality rises, the fruits of the work that is done and the resources produced are both more fairly and more widely distributed. People work better when they are working towards a common good. There is a greater sense of purpose. Shared prosperity unites a community, a city and a nation. The purpose of economic life is reoriented towards increasing *general* wellbeing, not the selfish individualist amassing of wealth and power by a lucky, selfish few.

We will know that the fall in inequalities is happening and becoming institutionalized when we *don't* see the people who can employ the most expensive lawyers always winning, when bankers who break the law are imprisoned and when sanctions are not used to coerce the poor into taking any work on offer. More equitable countries proudly and consistently support people in need of help, including those fleeing from danger and persecution. Economically unequal countries are far more likely to build walls and to refuse to take their share of refugees.

123

When Will the Fall in Inequality Become Clear?

When inequalities fall worldwide there will be fewer refugees, fewer wars and less destitution. The world's first global war, World War I, began in the year when economic inequalities last peaked. Rich countries that tolerate high economic inequalities also foster the greatest arms industries in the world. Everything is related and so there is no neat answer, but there are patterns. When economic inequalities last fell we saw the gaining of other rights that the wealthy had wanted to keep largely to themselves: voting rights, civil rights, rights to housing, health care and even the right of access to the countryside.

Discrimination on the grounds of race, religion, sexuality, gender and disability were all once considered justified by the better-off. Even when technically illegal, it takes increasing financial equality to actually eliminate such discrimination in practice. When equality has risen in the past, political systems have become both fairer and more fully representative. Everyone is far more able to have a voice and every vote is made to count. Electoral outcomes can less easily be engineered by wealthy lobbyists.

Decisions are taken at more appropriate levels. Democratic participation is more common and people are better connected to each other. The information needed to make meaningful democratic choices is better provided; political debate is more honest, accessible and inclusive. Education, the necessary foundation to all this, is a more joyful process, encouraging children to engage with enthusiasm, and adults to continue learning throughout their lives, but not just to undertake further study because they feel threatened in the job market by younger people with more qualifications.[40]

In the UK, if we wished to reduce the inequalities that educational divides create we would limit and reduce private funding of schooling and end or reduce all forms of segregation in primary and secondary education. We would also better recognize that in part inability, such as school failure, has been manufactured through providing poor quality education to poorer districts, the working classes and minorities.

Poor education is a precondition for maintaining high rates of inequality.[41] Large classes, stressed, poorly paid teachers in underfunded schools result in poor educational achievement that is then used as a justification for financial inequality. Just because a job does not require a degree, does not mean it is not worthwhile and deserving of just reward. If it is not worthwhile, why does anyone have to do it?

More equitable countries are more open to new ideas and information. They truly value creativity, research and discovery, rather than pretending to but actually worshipping profit. Companies do not talk about their prime responsibility being to their shareholders, but to their staff, their customers and to the community. The oligarchs and elitists are seen for what they are, little different from everyone else, just greedier.

In 2015 an American professor of philosophy tried to write a book arguing that inequality was not the problem. It was reviewed in the right-wing English magazine *The Spectator*. The reviewer concluded that apart from the high quality paper that the book was printed on, and the nice use of fonts, it was otherwise worthless.[42] It is when this reaction becomes commonplace that you know something has fundamentally changed.

Some argue that it takes a catastrophe to start the process of reducing inequality.[43] Others then cite a very long list of statistics that suggest that the catastrophe has already begun in the UK and started some time ago in the USA.[44] Today will appear catastrophic when it is looked back on from a future period of greater equality. But if the tide does not turn now towards greater equality, then today will appear wonderful compared to what is to come.

8

Reasons for Optimism

Success in business is often the result of luck, or of one or other kind of antisocial behaviour. This is rarely acknowledged by captains of industry. The greater their mediocrity, the greater their tendency to assume the success they enjoy must be due to their own outstanding talent, thus broadcasting to the world their lack of judgement. Far from being permitted to run a company, someone who thinks they've 'earned' £10m a year should be referred for psychiatric treatment.

Roger Carpenter, a Cambridge University
neurophysiologist, January 2017[1]

We have only very recently started to criticize those who advocate economic inequality as often and in as strong terms as Roger Carpenter's letter to a national newspaper cited above illustrates. Figure 1.1 in the first chapter of this book showed levels of inequality falling in the UK. Figure 1.3 showed them falling in most OECD countries. Figure 1.4 showed that the USA has now reached the point where a majority of adults aged under 40 can expect to be poorer than their parents if inequalities there are not reduced; and figure 1.5 in that chapter showed one slice of just how spatially divided by income London has again become. Where inequalities have risen most they have risen too high. The turn appears to have begun.

In the rest of this book, figure 2.1 showed that inequalities were highest in Holland when it was the richest country in the world, in 1732; highest in the UK when it was richest in 1802; and highest in the USA in 2010. Figure 2.2 showed incomes in the North American, Western European and most affluent Asian world regions converging downwards towards the world mean in recent decades. Figure 2.3 showed the gap between Nigeria and the UK shrinking even before the most acute years of the great recession. Figure 3.1 showed that inequality is currently both low and falling in Switzerland, Japan and the Netherlands. Figures 4.1 to 6.3 showed the unfairness and harm that high inequality produces. Figure 7.1 showed exports of luxury Swiss watches falling rapidly since 2015 and figure 7.2 warned of the huge rise to come in child poverty in the UK by 2021 unless inequalities are better addressed.

So much that we know now we did not know a decade ago. For instance, we should be optimistic because we now know economic insecurity harms innovation. If it did not there would be a case for inequality. The countries that became more unequal are now the least innovative. The USA did not become a land of milk and honey as a result of the entrepreneurship unleashed by Ronald Reagan's jump to the right. Donald Trump lambasted the US industrial record in his inaugural address, but as a property developer and speculator he had done nothing in his long business career to boost it.

Invention is a key part of raising productivity. Look again at the extent of inequality in 1983, and what happened a generation later to innovation. Of the twenty countries compared at various points in this book, Switzerland records by far the most patents per head (see figure 8.1). Of all those countries that file more than one intellectual property patent for every 10,000 people per year, the more equitable file more.[2] Patent filing records show Switzerland to be extreme, but to also fit the general pattern.[3] The least innovation is found in the states of the USA, especially in the most unequal of those states.

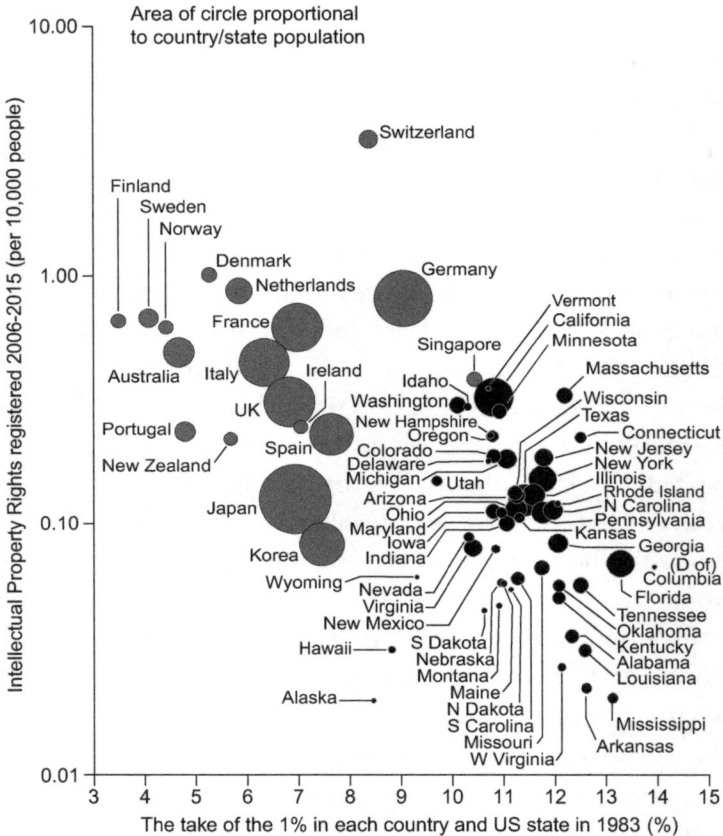

Figure 8.1 The take of the 1% in 1983 and IP patents per person in 2006–2015, 19 countries and all US states

Source: World Wealth and Income Database, http://wid.world/, accessed December 2016, patent data from the World Intellectual Property Organization (IPO) accessed December 2016, disaggregated by US state patent claims 2006–2015.
Note: Canada is not included because it is not a member of the Madrid IPO convention.

Reasons for Optimism

Just as inequality does not bolster innovation, it does not bolster measures to increase biodiversity and reduce crop monocultures. It does not encourage useful developments in finance. It does not create safe jobs. It does not promote brilliance, while greater equality does not result in mediocrity. In contrast, high economic equality goes hand in hand with governments working to encourage the reuse and recycling of goods rather than measuring their ever greater production and throwaway consumption as success.

Inequalities fall and innovation is greatest when education is free and student debt does not influence career choice; when all necessary health care is similarly free to access when needed and also does not result in the amassing of debt. The Swiss don't just produce the most patents in the world (per human head), they also spend the most on health care (per human body) in ways that are demonstrably effective, unlike the USA which spends highly on health with very little benefit on overall health.[4]

We should be optimistic because we are just beginning to realize that all speculative activities designed to make short-term profits at the expense of those who are duped could be regulated away. The Bank of England Chief Economist and the Executive Director of Monetary Analysis and

Statistics, Andy Haldane, discussed short-termism at length in a speech given at the University of Edinburgh Corporate Finance Conference in 2015. He suggested changing the law so that there is a minimum investment period in firms to discourage people playing the market.[5]

The importance of reducing inequality has risen greatly since 2010 in the public consciousness, as shown by figure 8.2 for the UK, although it is still dwarfed by the fear of immigration. It peaked in December 2016 when the film *I, Daniel Blake* was nominated for seven British Independent Film awards and won two.

We should be optimistic, because even in a country as unequal as the UK we are finally showing so many signs that we are now learning the true source of so many of our social problems. We will have seen inequality fall when we recognize that 'The greatest threat to our "way of life" is not migration.'[6] It will become difficult to understand why people ever thought migration was *the* key problem and shocking to learn that, in 2016, the UK refused admission to 3,000 unaccompanied refugee children out of the 24,000 in Europe that year.[7] Migrants tend to be the most innovative and productive of people, especially child refugees.[8]

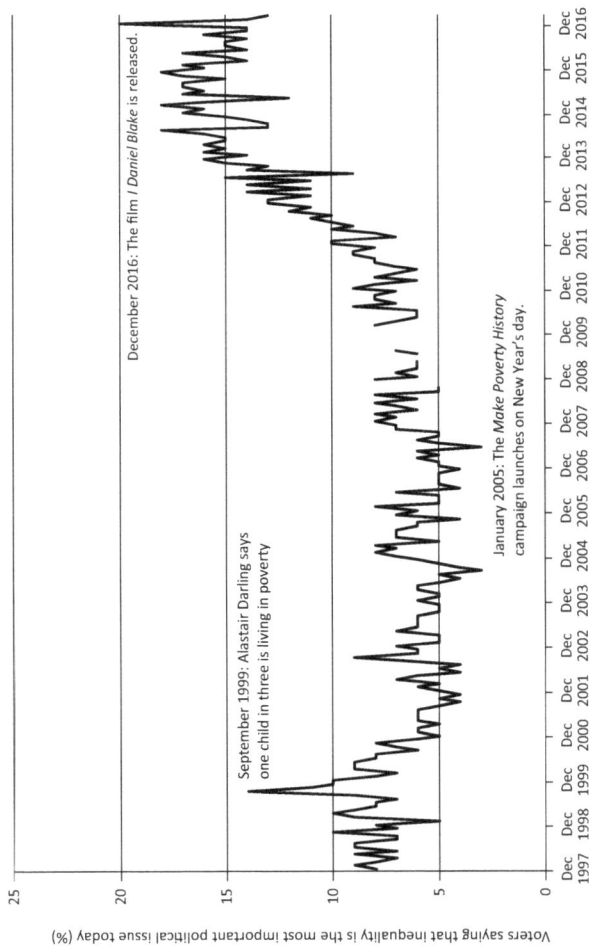

Figure 8.2 The importance of poverty and inequality, UK, 1998–2017

Source: Economist/Ipsos Mori Issues Index December 2016, http://www.slideshare.net/IpsosMORI/ipsos-mori-issues-index-december-2016. Reproduced with kind permission from Ipsos Mori who also supplied data for 2017, via Gideon Skinner and Michael Clemence.

People in economically unequal countries are encouraged by the media and by political parties to fear migrants rather than fearing those who amass wealth at others' expense and strenuously avoid paying taxes. Some people will always be much less concerned about inequality than others. Conservative voters are still less than half as likely to be concerned about inequality in the UK as compared to all other voters.[9] Ardent Conservatives differ in other ways, possibly including in how their brains have come to function.[10]

We have reasons to be optimistic about international tax avoidance. It is only because of the efforts of a few usually selfish individuals who try so hard to avoid paying their fair share of tax that tax avoidance is not better tackled. 'Coordination in the area of international taxation seems to have been blocked less by technical problems than by political lack of interest.'[11] Small Caribbean islands could be compensated for ceasing to be tax havens. This is because the amount of money rich countries lose to the tax havens is orders of magnitude greater than what the islands make from their low-tax regimes. More of these islands are British protectorates than come under any other jurisdiction. That is one of the reasons why the world's wealthy try so hard to keep Britain so unequal and out of the control of European courts.

Financial secrecy and very low or no inheritance taxes compound the growth of inequality. It may well be true that: 'The financial elite now float beyond national borders and no longer care about the welfare state, the common good, or for that matter any institution not subordinated to the dictates of finance capitalism.'[12] But they are few and they can only float because we, especially the British, let them. Their propaganda – that everyone else should have to tighten their belts – *indefinitely* – has a short shelf life after the plausibility wears off.

Austerity in the USA and UK is now seen as a 'fetishistic self-flagellation imposed on the majority in order to guarantee that the super-rich minority were not inconvenienced too much, and could rest assured that with every passing year their wealth would continue to grow'.[13] But change is in the air. In 2016 a major asset management firm, Hermes Investment Management, proposed a 40% cut in the average pay of FTSE 100 chief executives from £5m a year to £3m.[14] Then BlackRock, the world's largest investment firm, stated in 2017 that it would *not* support rises above average worker pay rises for the bosses of all the firms in which they had a major investment stake.[15] However it has also employed

135

the former UK Chancellor George Osborne on a salary of £650,000 a year for four days' work a month, so it is not practising what it preaches, but at least it now has to preach and others are now practising.

In Scotland the Scottish government funded a group called Poverty Alliance to promote the take-up of the living wage accreditation scheme across all of Scotland. By 2016, 439 Scottish employers were accredited.[16] Furthermore, Scotland aims to bring into force the socio-economic duties in the UK Equality Act 2010[17] before the rest of the UK does. It is in this part of the UK that calls for equality are growing most strongly, but there are wider trends and international trends that can be seen to matter more and more. We are only just learning all of what goes so badly wrong when high inequality is tolerated.

In 2016 the UK Co-operative Party called for a nationalization of social care, not via the model of the NHS but using genuinely co-operative not-for-profit local models: 'Our social care system is in urgent need of reform. Private companies profiteer, whilst older people, those who rely on social care and the staff that deliver it, pay the price. The market in social care services is broken incentivising a race to the bottom on quality and workforce conditions, a lack of accountability, and de-personalisation of services.'[18]

The current UK Chancellor (as I write), Philip Hammond, made his personal fortune through private care home profits. In March 2017 the UK Institute and Faculty of Actuaries announced that since 2011 life expectancy had ceased improving in the UK and also that inequalities between better-off people with defined contribution pensions and the rest were now rising.[19] Of all the countries of Europe, the UK was the only one to record no increase in life expectancy between 2011 and 2015; and it is the most economically unequal. This may be terrible news for the UK but it demonstrates to people in the rest of the world what happens when you allow inequalities to rise and rise. In even more inequitable USA, life expectancy is already falling (see chapter 5).

Inequality has been with us for the past 10,000 years, but so have times of rising equality, the despatching or emasculation of monarchs, the abolition of slavery, and the fall of empires. An exhaustive study of inequality worldwide and historically, from archaeological and anthropological perspectives, concluded that inequality is not inevitable, not genetic, not due to population pressure or environmental stress, but is usually due to the temporary adoption of new forms of 'social logic' that both justify and amplify it.[20]

Inequality has been and can be overcome by reversing the processes, the 'logic', that initially led to its rise, and not necessarily through resorting to violence.[21] We are becoming far less violent as a species, especially in those countries that first became most equal and have sustained those equalities. We now appear to be innovating and reversing the logic of our times, but not yet in the UK or USA – where there is currently least hope, but where we should still be hopeful, not least because of what is now happening both within these countries and around them.

Within the UK and USA a majority of young people have been (or are about to be) educated to university level. It will be extremely hard to convince this generation of young adults that they are all as worthless as the wages and benefits that most of them will receive will in future imply. For those without extremely rich parents, the vast majority will have huge student debts to pay back. Without greater future income equality they have no hope of a good life. They face juggling ever higher rents with more and more debt repayments. The majority of these graduates in both countries are women – educated, soon-to-be angry women.

Internationally inequalities are lower in almost all other rich countries worldwide and are currently falling in a majority of them. World population growth is not just slowing but the rate of that slow-down is accelerating as equalities also increase in the majority of poorer countries of the world. There will be fewer poorer young people to exploit world-wide in a generation's time, and rich countries are no longer able to maintain their income inequalities by robbing so much from the masses in other coun-tries to keep their rich so well off at home.[22]

It is always just before a housing market crash that people most ardently believe that prices cannot fall in the near future, which is why they then spend so much they push prices to their peak. It is when economic inequalities are at their highest that the least hope is evident, which is why there is always insufficient opposition to inequality rising to its highest peak, until that peak is seen to have passed. Inequality then falls continuously because once the logic that justified the highest wages is broken, any small reduction in greed at the top is not enough of a reduction.

In the UK today there are copious signs of the peak having been reached. On 4 April 2017, the newly appointed Commissioner of the London Metropolitan Police insisted on being paid £40,000 a year less than her predecessor.[23] On 6 April, it became law that all firms in the UK employing more than 250 people had to report their gender pay gaps.[24] Most early 2017 newspaper reports about the extent of pay inequalities did not mention that inequalities are just starting to fall, they just said they were still too high. Progress is now apparent, if grudging. In earlier decades those who argued against inequality were initially called sanctimonious, and only later seen as heroes.

Many decades ago, long before inequalities in the USA rose, the Swedish politician, economist and social scientist Gunnar Myrdal tried to explain to Americans the dangers of not holding inequality low.[25] He was later described as that 'sanctimonious Swede who has been paid well for telling us what's wrong with our country for a generation now'.[26] Given the subsequent diverging social and economic trends between Sweden and the USA, perhaps it was an error to call him sanctimonious. He was simply insightful.

Encouraging inequality feeds 'a coherent and totalitarian project based on relations of depredation, dispossession and exploitation, sustained by regulated privilege and geared to capital and power accumulation in the hands of a few'.[27] It is not that we just don't need inequality. It is that economic inequality is intensely destructive, not just to our societies but to our imaginations.[28]

Today it is when inequality falls that whole countries actually progress. There is now mounting evidence that since 2008 income inequalities in China have begun to fall and the benefits of prosperity have started to spread.[29] Today the World Wealth and Income Database reports the 1% taking a little less than they took a few years ago in the USA, South Africa, UK, Canada, China, Germany, Ireland, Switzerland, Australia, Italy, Japan, France, Spain, Norway, Finland and the Netherlands. Among all the countries enumerated in that database, only in Denmark, Sweden and New Zealand are inequalities higher at the most recent year of recording than they were in 2007 (see table 8.1).

When inequality is high people lose face, they lose confidence, they suffer from comparisons in which it is implied that the vast majority warrant little or no respect. Improvements in life expectancy stall or even reverse, you fear for your children and their future. Life feels like a game of chance with most of the odds heavily stacked against you. Fear divides one from another; loneliness increases, even as we become more crowded in cities. Our greatest fear is other people, and inequality becomes the enemy between us.

Table 8.1 The take of the 1% (percentage of all income), 2007–2015

	2007	2008	2009	2010	2011	2012	2013	2014	2015
USA	18.33	17.89	16.68	17.45	17.47	18.88	17.54	17.85	
South Africa	18.12	17.87	16.74	16.77	16.68				
UK	15.44	15.42	12.55	12.93	12.7				
Singapore	14.06	15.15	13.66	13.39	13.85	13.57			
Canada	13.72	13.06	12.29	12.22					
Germany	12.93	13.89	13.13	13.13					
China	12.3	12.3	12.2	12.0	12.0	11.4	11.6	11.4	11.4
Ireland	11.64	10.48	10.5						
Korea	11.28	11.37	11.33	11.76	12.25	12.23			
Switzerland	10.91	10.96	10.54	10.63					
Australia	10.06	9.84	8.59	8.88	9.17				
Italy	9.86	9.66	9.38						

Table 8.1 Continued

	2007	2008	2009	2010	2011	2012	2013	2014	2015
Japan	9.64	**9.71**	9.56	9.51					
France	**9.09**	8.51	7.78	8.11	9.27	8.94			
Spain	**9.03**	8.74	8.52	8.14	8.53	8.2			
Norway	**8.54**	7.7	7.11	7.74	7.8				
Finland	**8.26**	8.5	7.46						
New Zealand	7.83	8.11	7.84	7.4	8.16	**8.85**			
Netherlands	7.57	6.76	6.43	6.45	6.33	6.33			
Sweden	6.91	7.09	6.72	6.91	7.02	7.13	**7.24**		
Denmark	6.12	6.05	5.44	**6.41**					

Source: World Wealth and Income Database, http://wid.world/, accessed December 2016. China added April 2017.
Note: Year of highest take shown in bold text for each country.

Where inequalities have risen the most, the rich are terrified both of becoming poorer and of the poor. The poor and everyone in between cannot believe how much the rich waste. Great economic inequalities rose at the end of both the nineteenth and twentieth centuries as the greedy few took advantage of the confusion created by great social change. This was not because their huge greed was needed, but because it was not well enough understood and so not well enough controlled.

Today the pace of social change is slowing, global populations are stabilizing,[30] and we better understand the pathology of greed. We should not be surprised to see economic inequalities slowly fall. Children aged between 8 and 14 today could live all of their working lives in countries becoming more and more equal, as most of their great-grandparents did.[31] The alternative is catastrophe. But even if that is our fate, most catastrophes end with economic inequalities reducing. None of us can any longer afford the extent of inequality we currently tolerate – and be safe.

Notes

Chapter 1   Bell Curves

1 By William Shakespeare written 1603 or 1604.
2 Here all dollars are US dollars fixed to 1990 prices, see: Bolt, J. and van Zanden, J. L. (2014) The Maddison Project: collaborative research on historical national accounts, *The Economic History Review*, 67, 3, pp. 627–51. The Maddison-Project, http://www.ggdc.net/maddison/maddison-project/home.htm, 2013 version.
3 See figure 2.1 in this book for the best contemporary estimates of the very long-term trends in income inequalities for three of what were each once the most affluent nations on earth.
4 Alfani, G. (2017) *The Top Rich in Europe in the Long Run of History (1300 to present day)*, London: Centre for Economic Policy Research, http://voxeu.org/article/europe-s-rich-1300
5 Dorling, D. (2017) Are the rich really getting poorer and the poor getting richer? *The Conversation*, 11 January,

https://theconversation.com/are-the-rich-really-get ter-poorer-and-the-poor-getting-richer-71124

6 Oxfam (2017) *An Economy for the 99%: it's time to build a human economy that benefits everyone, not just the privileged few*, Oxford: Oxfam, http:// policy-practice.oxfam.org.uk/publications/an-econo my-for-the-99-its-time-to-build-a-human-economy-t hat-benefits-everyone-620170

7 Possibly the first bell curve to be applied to people appeared in Pearson, K. (1895) Contributions to the mathematical theory of evolution. II. Skew variation in homogeneous material, *Philosophical Transactions of the Royal Society of London, Series A*, Mathematical, 186, pp. 343–414, figure 17, plate 13. See Dorling, D. (2015) *Injustice*, Bristol: Policy Press, pp. 116–17.

8 McGuinness, F. (2016) *Income Inequality in the UK*, House of Commons Library Briefing Paper No. 7484, 24 November, http://researchbriefings.parliament.uk/ ResearchBriefing/Summary/CBP-7484

9 For example, see table 6 in Bellù, L. G. (2006) *Inequality Analysis: the Gini index*, http://www.fao. org/docs/up/easypol/329/gini_index_040EN.pdf. See also Gastwirth, J. L. (2014) Median-based measures of inequality: reassessing the increase in income inequality in the U.S. and Sweden, *Statistical Journal of the IAOS*, 30, pp. 311–20.

10 Konnikova, M. (2016) America's surprising views on income inequality, *The New Yorker*, 17 November, http://www.newyorker.com/science/maria-konniko va/americas-surprising-views-on-income-inequality

11 Leonhardt, D. (2016) The American Dream, quantified at last, *New York Times*, 8 December, http://www.nytimes.com/2016/12/08/opinion/the-american-dream-quantified-at-last.html

12 Davidai, S. and Gilovich, T. (2015) Building a more mobile America – one income quintile at a time, *Perspectives on Psychological Science*, 10, 1, pp. 60–71, https://research.chicagobooth.edu/~/media/5cc3cf051e5f428c90814fc5a480c05f.pdf

13 Americans, alongside other people who have grown up in very economically unequal countries, are among the worst at maths in the rich world by age 24. See Stotesbury, N. and Dorling, D. (2015) Understanding income inequality and its implications: why better statistics are needed, *Statistics Views*, Abingdon: Wiley, http://www.statisticsviews.com/details/feature/8493411/Understanding-Income-Inequality-and-its-Implications-Why-Better-Statistics-Are-N.html

14 Davidai and Gilovich, op. cit., p. 17.

15 Alesina, A., Di Tella, R. and MacCulloch, R. (2004) Inequality and happiness: are Europeans and Americans different? *Journal of Public Economics*, 88, pp. 2009–42, http://www.nber.org/papers/w8198.pdf

16 Dorling, D. and Thomas, B. (2016) *People and Places: a 21st-century atlas of the UK*, Bristol: Policy Press.

17 *Middle Layer Super Output Areas*, a level of UK government neighbourhood statistics with average populations of 7,500 and often with much housing

of similar tenure and type, https://www.ons.gov.uk/peoplepopulationandcommunity/personalandhouseholdfinances/incomeandwealth/articles/smallareamodelbasedincomeestimatesenglandandwales/financialyearending2014

18 Burgess, S. (2016) Revisiting changes in ethnic segregation in England's schools, Working Note, 19 September, http://simonburgesseconomics.co.uk/wp-content/uploads/2016/09/change-in-seg-20160919.pdf

19 Bateman, T. (2017) Independent school students gain extra time for exams, *BBC News*, 10 February, http://www.bbc.co.uk/news/education-38923034

20 Crawford, C., Dearden, L., Micklewright, J. and Vignoles, A. (2016) Unequal lives – to university and beyond, *Reclaiming Schools*, 16 December, https://reclaimingschools.org/2016/12/16/unequal-lives-to-university-and-beyond/

21 Dorling, D. (2017) *The Equality Effect: improving life for everyone*, Oxford: New Internationalist.

Chapter 2   A History of Inequality

1 Adichie, C. N. (2007) *Half of a Yellow Sun,* London: Fourth Estate, p. 23.

2 Lindert, P. and Williamson, J. (2016) *Unequal Gains: American growth and inequality since 1700,* Vox, CEPR Policy Portal, 16 June, http://voxeu.org/article/american-growth-and-inequality-1700

3 Power, S. (2017) From rage to revolution. *Unfair Economic Inequality and the Rise of Civic Discontent:*

remembering and deprivation in the Republic of Ireland, Cambridge: Cambridge University Press.

4 Field, P. (1999) The anti-roads movement: the struggle of memory against forgetting, in T. Jordan and A. Lent (eds) *Storming the Millennium: the new politics of change*, London: Lawrence & Wishart, pp. 68–79, at p. 74.

5 Bauman, Z. (2007) *Consuming Life*, Cambridge: Polity Press, p. 84, referring to Milan Kundera's novel *Slowness*. Milan Kundera originally wrote these words in *The Book of Laughter and Forgetting* in 1979.

6 Winston, G. (2014) Operation Legacy: how Britain destroyed thousands of colonial files, *War History Online*, 9 January, https://www.warhistoryonline.com/war-articles/operation-legacy-britain-destroyed-thousands-colonial-files.html

7 Cobain, I. (2016) *The History Thieves: secrets, lies and the shaping of a modern nation*, London: Portobello Books, p. 131.

8 Smith, T. (2013) Hanslope Park: home of Britain's 'real-life Q division', *The Register*, 5 July, http://www.theregister.co.uk/2013/07/05/geeks_guide_hanslope_park/

9 Cobain, op. cit., p. 124.

10 Ibid.

11 The 23% drop in the value of the Brazilian *Real* in 1999 and what pre-dated and post-dated it, https://en.wikipedia.org/wiki/Samba_effect

12 Sally Tomlinson (personal communication).

13 Oxfam (2016) A quarter of all new UK wealth goes to millionaires, Press release, 14 March,

http://www.oxfam.org.uk/media-centre/press-relea
ses/2016/03/a-quarter-of-all-new-uk-wealth-goes-to-
millionaires

14 Oxfam (2016) 62 people own same as half world,
Press release, 18 January, http://www.oxfam.org.uk/
media-centre/press-releases/2016/01/62-people-own-
same-as-half-world-says-oxfam-inequality-report-
davos-world-economic-forum; Oxfam (2017) Just
8 men own same wealth as half the world, Press
release, 16 January, https://www.oxfam.org/en/press
room/pressreleases/2017-01-16/just-8-men-own-
same-wealth-half-world

15 Szreter, S., Kinmonth, A. L., Kriznik, N. M. and Kelly,
M. P. (2016) Health, welfare, and the state – the dangers
of forgetting history, *The Lancet*, 288, pp. 2730–1.

16 Walsh, D., McCartney, G., Collins, C., Taulbut,
M. and Batty, G. D. (2016) *History, Politics and
Vulnerability: explaining excess mortality in Scotland
and Glasgow*, Glasgow Centre for Population Health,
NHS Health Scotland, the University of the West of
Scotland and University College London, p. 215.

17 Williams, A. (2016) What's behind the rise of anti-
establishment politics? From Brexit to Trump and
Bernie Sanders, frustration at inequality is rising –
and some experts think central bank policies are
to blame, *City AM*, 28 June, http://www.cityam.
com/244266/whats-behind-rise-anti-establishment-
politics-brexit-trump

18 *Finance Watch* (2016) Representation of the public
interest in banking, p. 35, http://www.finance-watch.
org/our-work/publications/1310

19 Pylas, P. (2017) World Economic Forum says capitalism needs urgent change, *The Washington Post*, 11 January, https://www.washingtonpost.com/world/europe/growing-gap-between-rich-and-poor-seen-as-key-economic-risk/2017/01/11/7e290a78-d7e3-11e6-a0e6-d502d6751bc8_story.html?

20 Hellebrandt, T. and Mauro, P. (2015) *The Future of Worldwide Income Distribution*, Working Paper 15-7, Washington, DC: Peterson Institute for International Economics, https://piie.com/publications/wp/wp15-7.pdf

Chapter 3   Why Argue for Inequality?

1 Frearson, A. (2016) Patrik Schumacher calls for social housing and public space to be scrapped, *Dezeen Magazine*, 18 November, https://www.dezeen.com/2016/11/18/patrik-schumacher-social-housing-public-space-scrapped-london-world-architecture-festival-2016/

2 The Mont Pèrelin Society is a forum for libertarian economists. It was created in 1947 at a conference in Mont Pèrelin, Switzerland, first organized by Friedrich Hayek, author of *The Road to Serfdom*.

3 See Diana Furchtgott-Roth's paper that 'documents the evolution of the feminist movement into a faction favoring redistribution, typically justified by a claim of wage discrimination that does not withstand statistical analysis', https://www.montpelerin.org/2016-general-meeting-miami-florida-papers/

4 Dorling, D. (2017) *The Equality Effect: improving life for everyone*, Oxford: New Internationalist.

5 Davies, W. (2014) How 'competitiveness' became one of the great unquestioned virtues of contempory culture, *LSE British Politics and Policy Blog*, 19 May, http://blogs.lse.ac.uk/politicsandpolicy/the-cult-of-competitiveness/

6 Rachman, G. (2017) Brexit reinforces Britain's imperial amnesia, *The Financial Times*, 27 March, https://www.ft.com/content/e3e32b38-0fc8-11e7-a88c-50b a212dce4d

7 Mann, G. (2017) *In the Long Run We Are All Dead: Keynesianism, political economy and revolution*, London: Verso, p. 363.

8 Tooze, A. (2017) America's political economy: leaving 50% behind, the very latest from Piketty, Saez and Co, *Adam Tooze Blog*, 9 February, https://www.adamtooze.com/2017/02/09/americas-political-econ omy-leaving-50-behind-latest-piketty-saez-co/

9 Narotzky, S. (2016) Between inequality and injustice: dignity as a motive for mobilization during the crisis, *History and Anthropology*, 27, 1, pp. 74–92, http://dx.doi.org/10.1080/02757206.2015.1111209

10 Drennan, M. P. (2015) *Income Inequality: why it matters and why most economists didn't notice*, New Haven, CT: Yale University Press.

11 Milanovic, B. (2016) Why global inequality matters, *Social Europe*, 18 March, https://www.socialeurope.eu/2016/03/why-global-inequality-matters/

12 Galbraith, J. K. (2016) *Inequality: what everyone needs to know*, Oxford: Oxford University Press.

13 Conley, D., Rauscher, E., Dawes, C., et al. (2013) Heritability and the equal environment assumption: evidence from multiple samples of misclassified twins, *Behaviour Genetics* 43, 5, pp. 415–26, http://link. springer.com/article/10.1007/s10519-013-9602-1; see also http://sociology.as.nyu.edu/docs/IO/41018/ twins_BG.pdf

14 Ibid., p. 417.

15 Silver, J. (2016) Look forward in anger, *The Guardian*, 14 November, https://www.theguardian. com/media/2005/nov/14/mailonsunday.monday mediasection

16 Snowdon, C. (2015) *Selfishness, Greed and Capitalism*, London: Institute of Economic Affairs, p. 184, http://iea.org.uk/sites/default/files/publications/ files/Selfishness,%20Greed%20and%20Capitalism. pdf

17 Frost, A. A. (2016) The declining taste of the global super-rich, *Current Affairs*, 25 March, https://www. currentaffairs.org/2016/03/the-declining-taste-of-the -global-super-rich

18 Hobbes, T. (1651) *Of Man, Being the First Part of Leviathan*, The Harvard Classics, chapter 13, http:// www.bartleby.com/34/5/13.html

Chapter 4   Who Benefits from Inequality?

1 Deaton, A. (2016) On death and money: history, facts, and explanations, *Journal of the American Medical Association*, 315, 16, pp. 1703–5, https:// www.ncbi.nlm.nih.gov/pubmed/27063421

2 Chetty, R., Stepner, M., Abraham, S., et al. (2016) The association between income and life expectancy in the United States, 2001–2014, *Journal of the American Medical Association*, 315, 16, pp. 1750–66. See also https://healthinequality.org/

3 Oxfam (2014) South Africa's two richest people have wealth equal to the poorest 26.5 million, *Radio 702 Blog*, 30 October, http://www.702.co.za/artic les/634/south-africa-s-two-richest-people-have-weal th-equal-to-the-poorest-26-5-million

4 Rapoza, K. (2016) In Brazil's local elections, the anti-vote wins, *Forbes Magazine*, 3 October, http://www.forbes.com/sites/kenrapoza/2016/10/03/in-brazils-local-elections-the-anti-vote-wins/#1b4c15aa71c8

5 *The Economist* (2005) The paradox of plenty, 20 December, http://www.economist.com/node/5323394

6 Corak, M. (2016) *Inequality from Generation to Generation: the United States in comparison*, IZA Discussion Paper 9929, May, http://ftp.iza.org/ dp9929.pdf

7 Ibid. The original diagram can be found at: https:// milescorak.com/2012/01/12/here-is-the-source-for-the-great-gatsby-curve-in-the-alan-krueger-speech-at-the-center-for-american-progress/

8 Friedman, S., Laurison, D. and Macmillan, L. (2017) *Social Mobility in Contemporary Britain: new insights from the Labour Force Survey*, London: Social Mobility Commission.

9 Clark, A. E., Flèche, S., Layard, R., et al. (2017) *The Origins of Happiness: how new science can transform our priorities*, Oxford: Princeton University Press.

10 Johnson, M. (2017) Letter: Fire the imagination — and the bean-counters, *The Guardian*, 2 January, https://www.theguardian.com/politics/2017/jan/01/fire-the-imagination-and-the-bean-counters

11 Jacoby, J. (2014) US legal bubble can't pop soon enough, *The Boston Globe*, 9 May, https://www.bostonglobe.com/opinion/2014/05/09/the-lawyer-bubble-pops-not-moment-too-soon/qAYzQ823qpfi4GQl2OiPZM/story.html

12 Weeks, J. F. (2014) *Economics of the 1%: how mainstream economics serves the rich, obscures reality and distorts policy*, London: Anthem Press.

13 Penzenstadler, N. and Page, S. (2016) Exclusive: Trump's 3,500 lawsuits unprecedented for a presidential nominee, *USA Today*, 6 January, http://www.usatoday.com/story/news/politics/elections/2016/06/01/donald-trump-lawsuits-legal-battles/84995854/

14 Bregman, R. (2017) *Utopia for Realists*, London: Bloomsbury, p. 105.

15 Sachs, J. (2016) The age of impunity, *The Boston Globe*, 13 May, https://www.bostonglobe.com/opinion/2016/05/12/the-age-impunity/LHBxamqFENCs3W6lvWnCIJ/story.html

16 Vulliamy, E. (2016) Mother asked for £10,500 wine budget in child maintenance case, *Microsoft News*, 14 March, http://www.msn.com/en-za/news/offbeat/mother-asked-for-%C2%A310500-wine-budget-in-child-maintenance-case/ar-AAgLnPx

17 Bowcott, O. and Booth, R. (2016) Tory donor's spending exposed in bitter divorce settlement, *The*

Guardian, 11 March, http://www.newslocker.com/en-uk/news/uk_news/tory-donors-spending-exposed-in-bitter-divorce-settlement/

18 Tomkinson, M. (2008) The UK's richest young entrepreneurs: top ten, *The Telegraph*, 21 February, http://www.telegraph.co.uk/finance/markets/2954731/The-UKs-richest-young-entrepreneurs-Top-ten.html

19 Rice, A. (2017) The young Trump: Jared Kushner is more like his father-in-law than anyone imagines, *New York Magazine*, 8 January, http://nymag.com/daily/intelligencer/2017/01/jared-kushner-trump-administration-power.html

20 Berton, B. (2012) Kushner comes back: Jared Kushner has been busy re-amassing his namesake company's multifamily portfolio in leaps and bounds, *Multifamily Executive*, 12 October, http://www.multifamilyexecutive.com/business-finance/transactions/kushner-comes-back_o

21 Sparke, M. (2016) Health and the embodiment of neoliberalism, in S. Springer, K. Birch and J. MacLeavey (eds) *The Handbook of Neoliberalism*, New York: Routledge, https://geography.washington.edu/publications/health-and-embodiment-neoliberalism

22 Hoxie, J. (2017) Health care repeal is a stealth tax break for millionaires, *Other Words,* 18 January, https://otherwords.org/health-care-repeal-is-a-steal-tax-break-for-millionaires/

23 Prince's Trust (2017) *The Prince's Trust Macquarie Youth Index for 2017*, London: Prince's Trust, https://www.princes-trust.org.uk/about-the-trust/research-policies-reports/youth-index-2017

24 Wilkinson, R. and Pickett, K. (2010) *The Spirit Level: why equality is better for everyone*, London: Penguin.

25 Hacker, J. and Pierson, P. (2011) *Winner-Take-All Politics: how Washington made the rich richer – and turned its back on the middle class*, New York: Simon & Schuster, pp. 99–100.

Chapter 5   Where Do the Costs of Inequality Fall?

1 Sachs, J. D. (2016) US must transition to low-carbon energy, *The Boston Globe*, 20 November, https://www.bostonglobe.com/opinion/2016/11/20/ must-transition-low-carbon-energy/fTMoMoFaNIFI Yr4NBLYkhM/story.html

2 Chetty, R., Stepner, M., Abraham, S., et al. (2016) The association between income and life expectancy in the United States, 2001–2014, *Journal of the American Medical Association*, 315, 16, pp. 1750–66, https://healthinequality.org/documents/

3 Bernstein, L. (2016) U.S. life expectancy declines for the first time since 1993, *The Washington Post*, 8 December, https://www.washingtonpost.com/nat ional/health-science/us-life-expectancy-declines-for-the-first-time-since-1993/2016/12/07/7dcdc7b4-bc9 3-11e6-91ee-1adddfe36cbe_story.html

4 Al-Agba, N. (2016) Does life expectancy matter?, *Health Care Blog*, 12 December, http://thehealth careblog.com/blog/2016/12/12/does-life-expectancy-matter/

5 Guo, J. (2017) The disease killing white Americans goes way deeper than opioids, *The Washington Post*,

24 March, https://www.washingtonpost.com/news/wonk/wp/2017/03/24/the-disease-killing-white-americans-goes-way-deeper-than-opioids/

6 West, D. (2016) Rocketing death rate sparks call for national investigation, *Nursing Times*, 17 February, https://www.nursingtimes.net/news/news-topics/public-health/rocketing-death-rate-sparks-call-for-national-investigation/7002500.article

7 Mundasad, S. (2016) Large 'jump in deaths' expert warns, *BBC News*, 16 February, http://www.bbc.co.uk/news/uk-england-35589564

8 Loopstra, R., McKee, M., Katikireddi, S. V., et al. (2016) Austerity and old-age mortality in England: a longitudinal cross-local area analysis, 2007–2013, *Journal of the Royal Society of Medicine*, 109, 3, pp. 109–16.

9 Jarman, B., Gault, S., Alves, B., et al. (1999) Explaining differences in English hospital death rates using routinely collected data, *British Medical Journal*, 318, 5 June, pp. 1515–20.

10 ONS (2016) *Measuring National Wellbeing: life in the UK: 2016*, London: Office for National Statistics. On the proportion of children with ill health see link to: https://www.ons.gov.uk/peoplepopulationandcommunity/wellbeing/datasets/childrenswellbeingmeasures

11 Razak, F., Davey Smith, G. and Subramanian, S. V. (2016) The idea of uniform change: is it time to revisit a central tenet of Rose's 'Strategy of Preventive Medicine'? *American Journal of Clinical Nutrition*, 104, 6, pp. 1497–507, https://www.ncbi.nlm.nih.gov/pubmed/27935518

12 McCann, K. (2016) Inheritance tax windfall for Treasury after winter death rates soar, *The Telegraph*, 18 March, http://www.telegraph.co.uk/finance/person alfinance/pensions/12197545/Inheritance-tax-windfall-for-Treasury-after-winter-death-rates-soar.html

13 Knapton, S. (2017) Flu jab blunder brought unexpected benefits for Britain's pension black hole, *The Telegraph*, 29 March, http://www.telegraph.co.uk/science/2017/03/29/flu-jab-blunder-brought-unexpec ted-benefits-britains-pension/; Cumbo, J. (2017) Life expectancy shift 'could cut pension deficits by £310bn', *The Financial Times*, 4 May, https://www.ft.com/content/77fa62fe-2feb-11e7-9555-23ef 563ecf9a

14 Tokudome, S., Hashimoto, S. and Igata, A. (2016) Life expectancy and healthy life expectancy of Japan: the fastest graying society in the world, *Bio Med Central Research Notes*, 9, p. 482, https://bmcresnotes.biomedcentral.com/articles/10.1186/s1 3104-016-2281-2

15 Bywaters, P., Bunting, L., Davidson, G., et al. (2016) *The Relationship Between Poverty, Child Abuse and Neglect: an evidence review*, York: Joseph Rowntree Foundation, https://www.jrf.org.uk/report/relationsh ip-between-poverty-child-abuse-and-neglect-evidence -review

16 Eckenrode, J., Smith, E., McCarthy, M. and Dineen, M. (2014) Income inequality and child maltreatment in the United States, *Paediatrics*, 133, 3, pp. 454–61, at p. 454, http://pediatrics.aappublications.org/cont ent/early/2014/02/04/peds.2013-1707

17 Bothwell, E. (2016) Fifth of Canadian students diagnosed with anxiety, *The Times Higher*, 13 September, https://www.timeshighereducation.com/news/fifth-canadian-students-diagnosed-anxiety

18 Galanti, M. R., Hultin, H., Dalman, D., et al. (2016) School environment and mental health in early adolescence – a longitudinal study in Sweden (KUPOL), *BMC Psychiatry*, 16, 243, table 4, http://bmcpsychiatry.biomedcentral.com/articles/10.1186/s12888-016-0919-1

19 Thomson, D. and Weston, G. (2017) 2 richest Canadians have more money than 11 million combined, CBC News, 15 January, http://www.cbc.ca/news/business/oxfam-davos-report-canadians-wealth-1.3937073

20 Child Poverty Action Group (2016) New figures reveal nearly half of children are living in poverty in some parts of the UK, 8 November, http://www.endchildpoverty.org.uk/new-figures-reveal-nearly-half-of-children-are-living-in-poverty-in-some-parts-of-the-uk/

21 Atkinson, T. (2015) *Inequality*, Cambridge, MA: Harvard University Press.

22 Pickett, K. and Wilkinson, R. (2017) Our collective failure to reverse inequality is at the heart of a global malaise, *British Medical Journal*, 356, j556, http://www.bmj.com/content/356/bmj.j556

23 Ryan, F. (2016) Five stories buried by Brexit, *The Guardian*, 7 July, https://www.theguardian.com/commentisfree/2016/jul/07/stories-buried-brexit-child-poverty-un-austerity and http://www.disabilitynewsservice.com/ministers-hid-secret-death-reports-from-their-fitness-for-work-test-reviewer/

24 Merrill, J. (2013) Hungry in Cameron's Cotswolds: beyond the 4x4s and classy shops of the PM's own constituency, a food bank is alarmingly busy, *The Independent*, 22 December, http://www.inde pendent.co.uk/news/uk/politics/hungry-in-camerons-cotswolds-beyond-the-4x4s-and-classy-shops-of-the-pms-own-constituency-a-food-9020229.html

25 Foster, D. (2016) Theresa May is no breath of fresh air on poverty, *The Guardian,* 19 July, https://www.theguardian.com/global/2016/jul/19/theresa-may-no-breath-fresh-air-poverty

26 Butler, P. (2016) Who knows how many people are going hungry? The government should, *The Guardian*, 20 April, https://www.theguardian.com/society/2016/apr/20/people-going-hungry-govern ment-food-insecurity

27 Galea, S. and Vaughan, R. (2017) A public health of consequence: review of the January 2017 issue of AJPH, *American Journal of Public Health*, 107, 1, p. 17, http://ajph.aphapublications.org/doi/abs/10.2 105/AJPH.2016.303540?af=R&

28 For the trends since 1900: Garrett, T. A. (2006) *100 Years of Bankruptcy: why more Americans than ever are filing*, Federal Reserve Bank of St Louis, https://www.stlouisfed.org/publications/bridges/spring-2006/100-years-of-bankruptcy-why-more-americans-than-ever-are-filing; and for the 2006–14 trend: http://www.bankruptcyaction.com/USbankstats.htm

29 Tugwell, P., Robinson, V. and Morris, E. (2007) Mapping global health inequalities: challenges and opportunities, *The Minority Health and Health*

Equity Archive, 19 May, http://health-equity.pitt.edu/896/

30 Walasek, L. and Brown, G. D. A. (2015) Income inequality and status seeking: searching for positional goods in unequal U.S. states, *Psychological Science*, 26, 4, pp. 527–33, quote at p. 529.

31 Bertrand, M. and Morse, A. (2013) *Trickle-Down Consumption*, NBER Working Paper No. 18883, http://www.nber.org/papers/w18883

32 Adkisson, R. V. and Saucedo, E. (2012) Emulation and state-by-state variations in bankruptcy rates, *The Journal of Socio-Economics*, 41, 4, pp. 400–7.

33 Christen, M. and Morgan, R. M. (2005) Keeping up with the Joneses: analyzing the effect of income inequality on consumer borrowing, *Quantitative Marketing and Economics,* 3, pp. 145–73, quote at p. 162.

34 Price Waterhouse Coopers (2016) Credit where it's due – UK unsecured borrowing increases by £62m a day, 3 November, http://pwc.blogs.com/press_room/2016/11/credit-where-its-due-uk-unsecured-borrowing-increases-by-62m-a-day.html

35 Hicks, D. L. and Hicks, J. H. (2014) Jealous of the Joneses: conspicuous consumption, inequality, and crime, *Oxford Economic Papers*, 66, pp. 1090–120, quote at p. 1090.

36 Heffetz, O. (2011) A test of conspicuous consumption: visibility and income elasticities, *Review of Economics and Statistics* 93, pp. 1101–17, quote at p. 1117, http://www.mitpressjournals.org/doi/pdf/10.1162/REST_a_00116

37 Santa Barbara County, Montecito Tourist Information Site (2017) No other town does luxury or exudes an effortlessly chic vibe like Montecito, http://santabarbaraca.com/explore-and-discover-santa-barbara/neighborhoods-towns/montecito/

38 Kenner, D. (2016) *Reducing Inequality and Carbon Footprints within Countries*, Working Paper, Global Sustainability Institute, February, http://whygreeneconomy.org/wp-content/uploads/2016/02/Kenner-2016.-Reducing-inequality-and-carbon-footprints-within-countries.pdf

39 Chancel, L. and Piketty, T. (2015) *Carbon and Inequality: from Kyoto to Paris. Trends in the global inequality of carbon emissions (1998–2013) & prospects for an equitable adaptation fund*, Paris School of Economics, 3 November, http://piketty.pse.ens.fr/files/ChancelPiketty2015.pdf

40 Hills, J. (2016) Super-rich paying less income tax despite HMRC 'crackdown', *ITV News*, 6 December, http://www.itv.com/news/2016-12-06/super-rich-paying-less-income-tax-despite-hmrc-crackdown/

41 Szreter, S. (2016) No, austerity clearly hasn't 'restored fairness' to the welfare system, *The Conversation*, 7 December, http://theconversation.com/no-austerity-clearly-hasnt-restored-fairness-to-the-welfare-system-69950

42 Chorley, M. (2016) Poorest families see a bigger slice of their income taken by the taxman than the richest people in Britain, *Daily Mail*, 30 June, http://www.dailymail.co.uk/news/article-3143197/Poorest-families-bigger-slice-income-taken-taxman-richest-people-Britain.html

43 Staff Reporter (2016) Five richest families in UK worth more than the poorest 20 per cent in society, *The Telegraph*, 17 March, http://www.telegraph.co.uk/news/10702213/Five-richest-families-in-UK-worth-more-than-the-poorest-20-per-cent-in-society.html

44 McDougall, J. (2016) No, this isn't the 1930s – but yes, this is fascism, *The Conversation*, 16 November, http://theconversation.com/no-this-isnt-the-1930s-but-yes-this-is-fascism-68867

45 Green, C. (2015) Scotland's four richest families 'worth £1 billion more than poorest 20% of population', *The Independent*, 7 October, http://www.independent.co.uk/news/uk/home-news/scotlands-four-richest-families-worth-1-billion-more-than-poorest-20-of-population-a6685411.html

46 Quilgars, D. and Pleace, N. (2016) Housing, living environments and life chances for children, in J. Tuckler (ed.) *Improving Children's Life Chances*, London: Child Poverty Action Group.

47 Stewart, K. (2016) Why we can't talk about life chances without talking about income, in J. Tuckler (ed.) *Improving Children's Life Chances*, London: Child Poverty Action Group.

48 Hooper, C., Gorin, S., Cabral, C. and Dyson, C. (2007) *Living with Hardship 24/7: the diverse experiences of families in poverty in England*, London: The Frank Buttle Trust, p. 58. http://www.york.ac.uk/admin/presspr/features/hardship.pdf

49 Clark, A., Fleche, S., Layard, R., et al. (2016) The big factors affecting life satisfaction are all non-economic, *LSE Business Review*, 12 December,

http://blogs.lse.ac.uk/businessreview/2016/12/12/
the-big-factors-affecting-life-satisfaction-are-all-non-
economic/

50 Tickle, L. (2016) How can it be right to have targets for
breaking up families? *The Guardian*, 13 December,
https://www.theguardian.com/commentisfree/2016/
dec/13/breaking-up-families-councils-child-adoptions

51 Mills, T. (2016) *The BBC: myth of a public service*,
London: Verso.

52 Schneider, M., Pottenger, M. and King, J. E. (2016)
The Distribution of Wealth: growing inequality?
Cheltenham: Edward Elgar, p. 180.

Chapter 6   What Are the Alternatives to Inequality?

1 Smith, Z. (2016) On optimism and despair, *The New
York Review of Books*, 22 December, http://www.
nybooks.com/articles/2016/12/22/on-optimism-and-
despair/

2 Pilgrim, D. (2012) The British welfare state and
mental health problems: the continuing relevance
of the work of Claus Offe, *Sociology of Health and
Illness,* 34, 7, pp. 1070–84.

3 NHS (2017) Mental health: support and guidance,
NHS Digital, http://content.digital.nhs.uk/mentalhealth

4 Mental Health Act Commission (2009) *Coercion
and Consent: monitoring the Mental Health Act
2007–2009*, London: The Stationery Office.

5 NHS Digital (2016) *Inpatients Formally Detained in
Hospitals under the Mental Health Act 1983, Annual
Statistics 2015/16*, 30 November, Leeds: Health and

Social Care Information Centre, http://www.content.digital.nhs.uk/catalogue/PUB22571/inp-det-m-h-a-1983-sup-com-eng-15-16-rep.pdf

6 Kobayashi, F. (2004) Job stress and stroke and coronary heart disease, *Journal of the Japan Medical Association*, 47, 5, pp. 222–6, http://www.med.or.jp/english/pdf/2004_05/222_226.pdf

7 Frank, R. (2017) *Success and Luck: good fortune and the myth of meritocracy*, Oxford: Princeton University Press.

8 Haushofer, J. and Fehr, E. (2014) On the psychology of poverty, *Science*, 344, 6186, pp. 862–7, https://www.princeton.edu/haushofer/publications/Haushofer_Fehr_Science_2014.pdf

9 Shoemaker, N. (2016) What happens when you give basic income to the poor? Canada is about to find out, *The Big Think*, 15 November, http://bigthink.com/natalie-shoemaker/canada-testing-a-system-where-it-gives-its-poorest-citizens-1320-a-month

10 Vanham, P. (2017) Davos leaders agree: share more wealth, or face the consequences, *World Economic Forum*, 20 January, https://www.weforum.org/agenda/2017/01/davos-leaders-agree-we-should-share-more-of-the-worlds-wealth-or-face-the-populist-consequences

11 Santens, S. (2017) Why we should all have a basic income, *World Economic Forum*, 15 January, https://www.weforum.org/agenda/2017/01/why-we-should-all-have-a-basic-income/

12 Goodman, P. (2017) Davos elite fret about inequality over vintage wine and canapés, *The New York Times*,

18 January, https://www.nytimes.com/2017/01/18/business/dealbook/world-economic-forum-davos-backlash.html?_r=1

13 Ibid.

14 Hardoon, D. and Slater, J. (2015) *Inequality and the End of Extreme Poverty: won't live with poverty, can't live with inequality*, Oxfam Media Briefing, 21 September, http://policy-practice.oxfam.org.uk/publications/inequality-and-the-end-of-extreme-poverty-577506

15 Sherman, E. (2016) These millionaires are begging New York state to raise their taxes, *Fortune Magazine*, 22 March, http://fortune.com/2016/03/22/millionaires-raise-taxes/

16 Silvestri, P. (2015) *Anthropology of Freedom and Tax Justice: between exchange and gift*, Working Paper 34/15, Department of Economics and Statistics, Torino (Italy), www.est.unito.it

17 Rutledge, R. B., de Berker, A.O., Espenhahn, S., et al. (2016) The social contingency of momentary subjective well-being, *Nature Communications*, 7, 11825, http://www.nature.com/articles/ncomms11825

18 Reynoulds, M. (2016) New 'happiness equation' links cheerfulness with equality, *Wired*, 14 June, http://www.wired.co.uk/article/happiness-equation-generosity-inequality-study

19 Sands, M. (2017) Exposure to inequality reduces support for redistribution, *Proceedings of the National Academy of Sciences*, 114, 4, pp. 663–8, http://scholar.harvard.edu/files/sands/files/pnas-2017-sands-1615010113.pdf

20 Cain Miller, C. (2017) Republican men say it's a better time to be a woman than a man, *The New York Times*, 17 January, https://mobile.nytimes.com/2017/01/17/upshot/republican-men-say-its-a-better-time-to-be-a-woman-than-a-man.html

21 Foa, R. S. and Mounk, Y. (2017) The signs of deconsolidation, *Journal of Democracy*, 28, 1, pp. 5–15, http://www.journalofdemocracy.org/sites/default/files/Foa%26Mounk%20-%20JoD%2028.1%20-%20PRE-PRINT%20VERSION.pdf

22 Aisch, G., Pearce, A. and Rousseau, B. (2016) How far is Europe swinging to the right? *New York Times*, 5 December, http://www.nytimes.com/interactive/2016/05/22/world/europe/europe-right-wing-austria-hungary.html

23 Madestam, A., Shoag, D., Veuger, S. and Yangizawa-Drott, D. (2013) Do political protests matter? Evidence from the Tea Party movement, *The Quarterly Journal of Economics*, 128, 4, pp. 1633–85.

24 Brickhill, C. (2016) *Singapore's Avaricious Oligarchy: the story of Singapore's despicable but desperate ruling top 1%*, Amazon Digital Services, https://www.amazon.co.uk/Singapores-Avaricious-Oligarchy-Despicable-Desperate/dp/153518275X

25 Rosenfield, A. and Schmeizer, E. (2016) Trump wins big in Wyoming, *The Caspar Star Tribune*, 8 November, http://trib.com/news/local/casper/trump-wins-big-in-wyoming/article_61ce99db-3e0b-5d34-96a0-ef0d83c098f1.html

26 Ellis, M. (2016) Traffic congestion isn't just annoying – it costs business £767 million each year, *Daily*

Mirror, 30 November, http://www.mirror.co.uk/
news/uk-news/traffic-congestion-isnt-just-annoying-9
362196

27 Reid, C. (2016) 'Rip out Embankment cycleway for
cash,' Chancellor tells London Mayor, *Bikebiz*, 21
November, http://www.bikebiz.com/news/read/rip-
out-parliament-s-cycleway-for-cash-chancellor-told-
london-s-mayor/020344

28 Focas, C. (2016) Travel behaviour and CO_2
emissions in urban and exurban London and New
York, *Transport Policy*, 46, pp. 82–91, http://www.
sciencedirect.com/science/article/pii/S0967070X153
00706

29 Darzi, A. (2017) London pollution: 'We are slowly
gassing ourselves to death – but we can change it',
The London Evening Standard, 20 February, http://
www.standard.co.uk/news/health/london-pollution-
we-are-slowly-gassing-ourselves-to-death-but-we-
can-change-it-a3469421.html

30 Bausells, M. (2016) Superblocks to the rescue:
Barcelona's plan to give streets back to residents, *The
Guardian*, 17 May, https://www.theguardian.com/
cities/2016/may/17/superblocks-rescue-barcelona-
spain-plan-give-streets-back-residents

31 Oxfam (2015) *Extreme Carbon Inequality*, Oxfam
Briefing, 2 December, https://www.oxfam.org/en/
research/extreme-carbon-inequality

32 Kennedy, B. (2017) Two-thirds of Americans give
priority to developing alternative energy over fossil
fuels, *Pew Research*, 23 January, http://www.
pewresearch.org/fact-tank/2017/01/23/two-thirds-

of-americans-give-priority-to-developing-alternative-
energy-over-fossil-fuels/

Chapter 7   When Will the Fall in Inequality Become Clear?

1 Narotzky, S. and Besnier, N. (2014) Crisis, value, and hope: rethinking the economy, *Current Anthropology*, 44, suppl. 9, pp. S4–S16, quote at p. S7.
2 World Wealth and Income Database, http://wid. world/, accessed 11 March 2017. See also Lu, J. (2017) China can still reverse inequality before it's as bad as the U.S., *Humanosphere Blog*, 17 February, http://www.humanosphere.org/basics/2017/02/chi na-can-still-reverse-inequality-bad-u-s/
3 Chandy, L. and Seidel, B. (2017) *How Much do we Really Know about Inequality within Countries around the World? Adjusting Gini coefficients for missing top incomes*, Working Paper, Brookings Institute, 17 February, https://www.brookings.edu/ opinions/how-much-do-we-really-know-about-inequ ality-within-countries-around-the-world/
4 Lansley, S. (2011) *The Cost of Inequality: three decades of the super-rich and the economy*, London: Gibson Square, p. 97.
5 Dolan, K. A. and Kroll, L. (2016) Forbes 2016 world's billionaires: meet the richest people on the planet, *Forbes Magazine*, 1 March, http://www. forbes.com/sites/luisakroll/2016/03/01/forbes-2016- worlds-billionaires-meet-the-richest-people-on-the- planet/#77ee391641cb

6 Vinton, K. (2017) African billionaire fortunes decline on new Forbes list of the continent's richest, *Forbes Magazine*, 9 January, http://www.forbes.com/sites/katevinton/2017/01/09/african-billionaire-fortunes-decline-on-new-forbes-list-of-the-continents-richest/#33c4c9f0363d

7 Wang, J. (2016) Donald Trump's fortune falls $800 million to $3.7 billion, *Forbes Magazine*, 28 September, http://www.forbes.com/sites/jenniferwang/2016/09/28/the-definitive-look-at-donald-trumps-wealth-new/#56731ce77e2d

8 Gilbert, M. (2016) Middle-class angst is depressing Swiss watch sales, *Bloomberg*, 12 December, https://www.bloomberg.com/view/articles/2016-12-12/middle-class-angst-is-depressing-swiss-watch-sales

9 Currid-Halkett, E. (2017) *The Sum of Small Things: a theory of the aspirational class*, Oxford: Princeton University Press.

10 Collinson, P. (2016) Sales of luxury London properties collapsed by 86% in past year, *The Guardian*, 17 October, https://www.theguardian.com/business/2016/oct/17/luxury-london-property-sales-collapse-developers-taxes

11 Anderson, S. (2016) This city just came up with a novel way to fight inequality: taxing corporations with extreme pay gaps, The Nation, 8 December, https://www.thenation.com/article/his-city-just-came-up-with-a-novel-way-to-fight-inequality-taxing-corporations-with-extreme-gaps-between-ceo-and-worker-pay/

12 Kerber, R. (2016) CEO-worker pay gap stays wide despite wage hikes: unions, Reuters press release,

17 May, http://www.reuters.com/article/us-usa-ceo-pay-idUSKCN0Y81S9

13 Worstall, T. (2016) Excellent news: top CEOs make 335 times the average American worker, *Forbes Magazine on-line comment*, 17 May, http://www.forbes.com/sites/timworstall/2016/05/17/excellent-news-top-ceos-make-335-times-the-average-american-worker/#50b420eb1c69

14 Petroff, A. (2016) U.K. could force companies to reveal worker-CEO pay gap, *CNN Money*, 29 November, http://money.cnn.com/2016/11/29/news/ceo-pay-gap-uk-income-inequality/

15 Jones, O. (2014) Owen Jones's 'Agenda for Hope': we want a fairer society – and here's how we can achieve it, *The Independent*, 26 January, http://www.independent.co.uk/voices/comment/owen-joness-agenda-for-hope-we-want-a-fairer-society-and-here-s-how-we-can-achieve-it-9086440.html

16 Hackett, P. and Clark, D. (2015) The left must think big to win, *New Statesman*, 8 April, http://www.newstatesman.com/politics/2015/04/left-must-think-big-win-big

17 Massey, D. and Rustin, M. (2013) Displacing neoliberalism, *Kilburn Manifesto*, *Soundings (A Journal)*, London: Lawrence and Wishart, p. 208, https://www.lwbooks.co.uk/sites/default/files/11_displacing neoliberalism.pdf

18 Personal Finance (2017) Buy-to-let mortgages pulled at fastest rate since 2009, *The Week*, 10 January, http://www.theweek.co.uk/66688/buy-to-let-mortgages-pulled-at-fastest-rate-since-2009

19 NEF (2008) *From the Ashes of the Crash: 20 first steps from new economics to rebuild a better economy*, London: New Economics Foundation, http://base.socioeco.org/docs/from_the_ashes_of_the_crash_1.pdf

20 Common Weal (2014) *The Key Ideas: economics and social equity, on-line manifesto of ideas 58 to 81*, Glasgow: Common Weal, http://www.allofusfirst.org/the-key-ideas/category/economic-and-social-equality/

21 EBA (2016) *EBA Reports on High Earners and the Effects of the Bonus Cap*, 30 March, London: European Banking Authority, http://www.eba.europa.eu/-/eba-reports-on-high-earners-and-the-effects-of-the-bonus-cap

22 Treanor, J. (2017) UK home to 80% of top-earning European bankers, *The Guardian*, 2 February, https://www.theguardian.com/business/2017/feb/02/european-bankers-uk-city-brexit-talks

23 Treanor, J. (2016) Nearly 1,000 city staff at four big US banks given €1m in pay deals in 2015, *The Guardian*, 28 December, https://www.theguardian.com/business/2016/dec/28/wall-street-banks-city-staff-executive-pay-bonuses-2015

24 EBA (2016) *Benchmarking of Remuneration Practices at the European Union Level and Data on High Earners* (data as of end 2014), London: European Banking Authority, https://www.eba.europa.eu/documents/10180/1359456/EBA+Op-2016-05++(Report+on+Benchmarking+of+Remuneration+and+High+Earners+2014).pdf

25 McGeever, J. and Davies, A. (2017) Number of newly-minted millionaires at Europe's big banks is shrinking, *Reuters*, 24 March, http://uk.reuters.com/article/us-investment-banks-millionaires-analysi-idU KKBN16V261

26 Kollewe, J. and Davies, R. (2016) Big rise in City bankers earning more than €1m, *The Guardian*, 30 March, http://www.theguardian.com/business/2016/mar/30/rise-number-city-financiers-uk-earning-mo re-than-1m

27 AFP (2017) Goldman Sachs moving London staff to Frankfurt due to Brexit: report, *The Local*, 19 January, https://www.thelocal.de/20170119/gold man-sachs-moving-london-staff-to-frankfurt-due-to-brexit-report

28 Nussbaum, A. (2017) Paris big dig abandons chic Haussmann for trains to the suburbs, *Bloomberg News*, 10 March, https://www.bloomberg.com/news/articles/2017-03-10/paris-big-dig-abandons-chic-haussmann-for-trains-to-the-suburbs

29 Brickhill, C. (2016) *Risk Traffickers: the story of how our bankers became bank robbers*, Amazon Open Concepts Publishing, pp. 306–8.

30 City and Financial Reporter (2016) Britain's highest paid chief executive, WPP's Martin Sorrell, pockets £65m as his pay rises by 63%, *Daily Mail*, 14 March, http://www.thisismoney.co.uk/money/markets/art icle-3490561/Britain-s-highest-paid-chief-executive-WPP-s-Martin-Sorrell-pockets-65m-pay-rises-63.html

31 Goldberg, E. (2014) The Giving Pledge is just a glorified tax break: critics, *The Huffington Post*,

13 February, http://www.huffingtonpost.com/2014/02/13/giving-pledge-critics_n_4776265.html

32 Dorling, D. (2017) Are the rich really getting poorer and the poor getting richer? *The Conversation*, 11 January, https://theconversation.com/are-the-rich-really-getting-poorer-and-the-poor-getting-richer-71124

33 ONS (2016) *Household Disposable Income and Inequality, financial year ending 2016*, London: Office for National Statistics, figure 3, https://www.ons.gov.uk/peoplepopulationandcommunity/personalandhouseholdfinances/incomeandwealth/bulletins/householddisposableincomeandinequality/financialyearending2016

34 Browne, J. and Hood, A. (2016) *Living Standards, Poverty and Inequality in the UK: 2015–16 to 2020–21*, Report 114, London: Institute for Fiscal Studies, figure 3.9, http://www.ifs.org.uk/publications/8171

35 Beatty, C. and Fothergill, S. (2016) *The Uneven Impact of Welfare Reform: the financial losses to places and people,* Sheffield: Sheffield Hallam University, Centre for Regional Economic and Social Research, https://www.shu.ac.uk/research/cresr/sites/shu.ac.uk/files/welfare-reform-2016_1.pdf

36 Hood, A. and Waters, T. (2017) *Living Standards, Poverty and Inequality in the UK: 2016–17 to 2021–22*, London: Institute for Fiscal Studies, figure 3.5, https://www.ifs.org.uk/uploads/publications/comms/R127.pdf

37 Traynor, L. (2015) Former detectives set up Britain's first private police force – costing residents £1 a

week, *The Mirror*, 16 January, http://www.mirror.co.uk/news/uk-news/former-detectives-set-up-britains-4992372

38 Garside, R. and Ford, M. (2016) *UK Justice Policy Review*, vol. 5, London: Centre for Crime and Justice Studies, pp. 18–19, https://www.crimeandjustice.org.uk/project/uk-justice-policy-review

39 Rector, K. (2017) Trump says 'carnage' in America 'stops right now.' How will that play out in Baltimore? *The Baltimore Sun*, 20 January, http://www.baltimoresun.com/news/maryland/crime/bs-md-trump-crime-20170120-story.html

40 Aniko Horvath (personal communication, March 2017).

41 Tomlinson, S. (2017) *A Sociology of Special and Inclusive Education: exploring the manufacture of inability*, London: Routledge.

42 Walther, M. (2015) The best thing about Harry G. Frankfurt's 'On Inequality' is the paper: the popular philosopher's 'response' to Thomas Piketty is pompous, trite and economically illiterate, *The Spectator*, 17 October, http://www.spectator.co.uk/2015/10/the-best-thing-about-harry-g-frankfurts-on-inequality-is-the-paper-its-printed-on/

43 Scheidel, W. (2017) *The Great Leveler: violence and the history of inequality from the Stone Age to the twenty-first century*, Oxford: Princeton University Press.

44 Wilkinson, R. and Pickett, K. (2017) Prepare for the worst: this inequality rift will tear our society apart, *The Guardian*, 3 February, https://www.the

guardian.com/commentisfree/2017/feb/03/prepare-inequality-rift-tear-society-apart-thatcher?

Chapter 8   *Reasons for Optimism*

1 Carpenter, R. (2017) Saints and sinners in the pay cap debate. Letters, *The Guardian*, 12 January, https://www.theguardian.com/money/2017/jan/12/saints-and-sinners-in-the-pay-cap-debate

2 European Patent Office (2016) *Filing 2006–2015 per Country of Residence of the Applicant*, https://www.epo.org/about-us/annual-reports-statistics/statistics.html#national

3 World IPO data for the Madrid Convention Registrations, http://ipstats.wipo.int/ipstatv2/searchForm and USA state patent data from here: https://www.uspto.gov/web/offices/ac/ido/oeip/taf/cst_utl.htm

4 Dorling, D. (2016) *A Better Politics: how government can make us happier*, London: London Publishing Partnership, http://www.dannydorling.org/books/betterpolitics/

5 Haldane, A. (2015) Who owns a company? Speech, http://www.bankofengland.co.uk/publications/Pages/speeches/2015/833.aspx

6 Penny, L. (2015) Europe shouldn't worry about migrants. It should worry about creeping fascism, *The New Statesman*, 14 August, http://www.newstatesman.com/politics/2015/08/europe-shouldn-t-worry-about-migrants-it-should-worry-about-creeping-fascism

7 Dubs, A. (2016) House of Lords Grand Committee, Immigration Bill, 9 February, http://www.publicati ons.parliament.uk/pa/ld201516/ldhansrd/text/1602 09-gc0001.htm

8 Ward, L. (2013) Kindertransport: 'To my dying day, I will be grateful to this country', *The Telegraph*, 26 May, http://www.telegraph.co.uk/history/britain-at-war/10080264/Kindertransport-To-my-dying-day-I-will-be-grateful-to-this-country.html

9 Skinner, G. and Clemence, M. (2017) *A Rise in Those Who Think the NHS and Poverty/Inequality Are Important Issues Facing Britain*, London: Ipsos Mori, https://www.ipsos-mori.com/researchpublications/researcharchive/3832/A-rise-in-those-who-think-the-NHS-and-povertyinequality-are-important-issues-facing-Britain.aspx

10 Haruno, M., Kimura, M. and Frith, C. D. (2014) Activity in the nucleus accumbens and amygdala underlies individual differences in prosocial and individualistic economic choices, *Journal of Cognitive Neuroscience*, 26, 8, pp. 1861–70.

11 Modlander, P. (2014) *The Anatomy of Inequality*, New York: Melville House Publishing, p. 180.

12 Giroux, H. (2015) Culture of cruelty: the age of neo-liberal authoritarianism, *Counter Punch*, 23 October, http://www.counterpunch.org/2015/10/23/culture-of-cruelty-the-age-of-neoliberal-authoritarianism/

13 Winlow, S., Hall, S. and Treadwell, S. (2017) *Rise of the Right*, Bristol: Policy Press, p. 20.

14 Treanor, J. (2016) Scrap bonuses? Fund manager looks into reforming executive pay, *The Guardian*, 14

October, http://www.theguardian.com/business/2016/oct/14/scrap-bonuses-fund-manager-reforming-executive-pay-hermes-investment-management

15 Monaghan, A. (2017) World's largest fund manager demands cuts to executive pay and bonuses, *The Guardian*, 16 January, https://www.theguardian.com/business/2017/jan/15/blackrock-demands-cuts-to-executive-pay-and-bonuses

16 Eisenstadt, N. (2016) *Shifting the Curve: a report for the Scottish government*, Edinburgh, http://www.gov.scot/Resource/0049/00492430.pdf

17 Equality and Diversity Forum (2016) Scottish Government commitment to Equality Act socio-economic duty, 9 June, http://www.edf.org.uk/blog/scottish-government-commitment-to-equality-act-socio-economic-duty/#

18 Scott, J. (2016) *Taking Care: a co-operative vision for social care in England,* Co-operative Councils Innovation Network, September, http://www.councils.coop/publications/taking-care-co-operative-vision-social-care-england/

19 Mortality Projections Committee (2017) *CMI Mortality Projections Model: CMI_2016*, Working Paper 97, London: Institute and Faculty of Actuaries, https://www.actuaries.org.uk/documents/summary-cmi-working-paper-97-cmi-mortality-projections-model-cmi2016

20 Bowles, S., Smith, E. A. and Borgerhoff-Mulder, M. (2010) The emergence and persistence of inequality in pre-modern societies, *Current Anthropology*, 51, pp. 7–17, https://faculty.washington.edu/easmith/

Bowles,Smith,Borgerhoff_Mulder_2010-CA-Intro.
pdf

21 Flannery, K. and Marcus, J. (2014) *The Creation of Inequality: how our prehistoric ancestors set the stage for monarchy, slavery and empire*, Boston: Harvard University Press.

22 Dorling, D. (2017) *The Equality Effect: improving life for everyone*, Oxford: New Internationalist.

23 Hamilton, F. (2017) Met chief takes a £40,000 pay cut to share police pain, *The Times*, 5 April, https://www.thetimes.co.uk/edition/news/met-chief-takes-a-40-000-pay-cut-to-share-police-pain-l6v5z366j

24 Lake, E. and Windle, L. (2017) Please mind the gap, *The Sun*, 6 April, https://www.thesun.co.uk/living/1657321/gender-pay-gap-new-reporting-regulations-gender-discrimination/

25 Myrdle, G. (1944) *The American Dilemma: the negro problem and modern democracy*, New York: Harper Brothers, https://en.wikipedia.org/wiki/An_American_Dilemma

26 Thanks to Simon Reid Henry for the reference, which was in turn cited in Jeanne Marie O'Toole (1992) *An Analysis of Gunnar Myrdal's Social and Educational Theory*, e-Commons Dissertations, Paper 1216, p. 40 http://ecommons.luc.edu/luc_diss/1216

27 Narotzky, S. (2016) On waging the ideological war: against the hegemony of form, *Anthropological Theory*, 16, 2–3, pp. 263–84, quote at p. 279.

28 Hughes, B. (2016) *The Bleeding Edge: why technology turns toxic in an unequal world*, Oxford: New Internationalist.

29 Zhuang, H. and Shi, L. (2016) *Understanding Recent Trends in Income Inequality in the People's Republic of China,* ADB Economics Working Paper Series, No. 489, July, Philippines: Asian Development Bank, https://www.adb.org/sites/default/files/publication/186143/ewp-489.pdf

30 Dorling, D. (2013) *Population 10 Billion*, London: Constable.

31 Dodgson, R. (2017) Fighting inequality and poverty requires a more humane view of economics, *The Conversation*, 30 January, https://theconversation.com/fighting-inequality-and-poverty-requires-a-more-humane-view-of-economics-71600